Epistemetrics

Epistemetrics is a scholarly discipline waiting to be born. With regard to scientific information there is the discipline of scientometrics, represented by a journal of that name. Science, however, does not have a monopoly on knowledge; although it is one of our most important cognitive resources, it is not our only one. While scientometrics is a centerpiece of epistemetrics, it is far from being the whole of it. Nicholas Rescher's endeavor to quantify knowledge is not only of interest in itself, but it is also instructive in bringing into sharper relief the nature of and the explanatory rationale for the limits that unavoidably confront our efforts to advance the frontiers of knowledge. In pursuing this objective, Rescher's book takes the measure of both the vast extent and the ultimate limitations of human knowledge.

Nicholas Rescher is University Professor of Philosophy at the University of Pittsburgh, where he is also Chairman of the Center for Philosophy of Science. He has received fellowships from the Ford, Guggenheim, and National Science Foundations. Author of more than one hundred books ranging over many areas of philosophy, he is the recipient of six honorary degrees from universities on three continents and was awarded the Alexander von Humboldt Prize for Humanistic Scholarship in 1984.

Epistemetrics

NICHOLAS RESCHER

University of Pittsburgh

CAMBRIDGE UNIVERSITY PRESS

Cambridge, New York, Melbourne, Madrid, Cape Town, Singapore, São Paulo

Cambridge University Press

40 West 20th Street, New York, NY 10011-4211, USA

www.cambridge.org

Information on this title: www.cambridge.org/9780521861205

First published 2006

Printed in the United States of America

A catalog record for this publication is available from the British Library.

Library of Congress Cataloging in Publication Data

Rescher, Nicholas.

Epistemetrics / Nicholas Rescher.

p. cm.

Includes bibliographical references and index.

ISBN 0-521-86120-9 (hardback)

1. Knowledge, Theory of. 2. Verification (Empiricism) I. Title.

BD212.5.R47 2006

121–dc22 2005019557

ISBN-13 978-0-521-86120-5 hardback

ISBN-10 0-521-86120-9 hardback

To James R. Wible

Contents

Preface

> When you can measure what you are speaking about, and express it in numbers, you know something about it; but when you cannot measure it, when you cannot express it in numbers, your knowledge is of a meager and unsatisfactory kind: it may be the beginning of knowledge, but you have scarcely, in your thoughts, advanced to the stage of *science*.
> – William Thomson, Lord Kelvin (1824–1907), English Physicist

This book develops the theory of knowledge from a quantitative perspective that serves to throw light on the scope and limits of human knowledge. It seeks to provide theorists of knowledge in philosophy, information theory, cognitive studies, communication theory, and cognate disciplines with the conceptual tools required for a quantitative treatment of the products of inquiry.

Kelvin's dictum is an exaggeration that takes things too far. I have never thought for a moment that if you cannot say it with numbers that it just is not worth saying. But all the same, I do firmly believe that where you cannot put numbers to work you will understand the matter better and more clearly for being able to explain why. So it seems well worthwhile to see what a qualitative approach to knowledge can do for us.

The discipline represented by the domain of inquiry to which the present book is addressed does not as yet exist. *Epistemetrics* is not yet a scholarly specialty. To be sure, as regards scientific information in specific there is the discipline of scientometrics, represented by a journal of that name. But while this book too will keep scientific knowledge in the foreground, various of its key principles – for example Duhem's Law of Chapter 1, or the Principle of Quality Retardation of Chapter 6 – hold every bit as much for our knowledge of everyday-life matters as they do for the natural and human sciences. After all, science does not have a monopoly on knowledge: while it is doubtless our most important cognitive resource it is not our *only* one. And so while scientometrics is a centerpiece of epistemetrics, it is not the whole of it.[1]

Again the measurement of *intelligence* is a large and flourishing industry. But intelligence is no more than the *capacity* for producing and handling knowledge and does not as such address the product itself. Then too there are all sorts of tests and quiz shows and even games (on the order of Trivial Pursuit) that compare the knowledge of different individuals. But of course such comparisons do not address the epistemetric issue of cognitive measurement at large. And so, seeing that epistemetrics is not as yet an established field of inquiry, the present discussion can do no more than offer a preliminary glimpse into the nature of such a discipline.

Autobiographically speaking, I now believe that my brief time of service at the RAND Corporation some 50 years ago convinced me of the power and utility of the quantitative point of view. And I am persuaded that it affords us the basis for a deeper understanding of the nature and prospects of the processes at issue with the accession and development of knowledge.

To be sure, many factors conspire to make the measurement of knowledge into a vexed and complicated enterprise. A head count of particular items of information is of course pointless because one item can informatively encompass many others. Thus someone who knows a general truth is in a position to infer all of its potentially innumerable instances. One generalization can encompass a zillion particularities. And this points to the further issue that information is not created equal – some items deal with large and important matters, some with trivialities.

Given such complications it may seem unexpected that anything instructive can be accomplished in the epistemetric project of quantifying knowledge. But something can indeed be done, and the

---

[1] My personal effort in the domain of scientometrics is represented by my *Scientific Progress* (Oxford: Blackwell, 1978). It will be obvious to anyone who knows that book that the present work is heavily indebted to it.

present discussion will endeavor to synthesize and coordinate some of the useful suggestions that have been offered along these lines over the years.

Rather surprisingly, epistemology, that is, the theory of *knowledge*, has generally not made much of the distinction between various modes of cognitively available material – between reasonable conjecture and plausible supposition, for example, or between reliable information and actual knowledge. But it is this latter distinction – between mere information and genuine knowledge – that is pivotal for the present deliberations, which will seek to address the qualitative issue of knowledge versus information in a quantitative perspective.

The book's venture into the quantification of knowledge will proceed by a series of principles which, for reasons of mnemonic vividness can be indicated by association with various scientists and philosophers. Sometimes their work suggests rather than formulates what is at issue. But no matter! For what matters more than historical piety is that the pieces all fit together to make up a coherent and cohesive story regarding the limitations of inquiry and the limits of knowledge.

Ironically, the business of cognitive quantification is so problematic that one could say with some justice that the present treatment of quantities is qualitative in nature, and that rather than providing a properly quantitative assessment of our knowledge it only offers a qualitative perspective on it. But even if that were so, such an exercise is instructive in bringing into sharper relief the nature of and the explanatory rationale for the limits that unavoidably confront our ongoing efforts to advance the frontiers of knowledge. And the quantitative perspective developed here – in however rough and sketchy a way – affords some instructive insights into the nature of cognition that no merely qualitative deliberations would make available. In particular, the project manages to throw some vivid light on the unavoidable limitations of human knowledge.

Erik Angner and C. J. Thomas read my manuscript and spotted various corrigenda. And I am grateful to Estelle Burris for her highly competent assistance in seeing the book through the process of getting into print.

Pittsburgh, Pennsylvania
May 2005

1

Asking for More Than Truth

Duhem's Law of Cognitive Complementarity

(1) Duhem's Law of cognitive complementarity holds that inquiry is subject to a complementary relationship between security and confidence on the one hand, and definiteness and detail on the other, so that s × d ≤ const. (2) Among other things, this relationship serves to characterize the difference between science and common sense, seeing that these two domains take a very different stance regarding security and definiteness. (3) Duhem's Law engenders an impetus to vagueness in matters where truth is paramount. (4) Moreover, security/detail complementarity has important lessons for the conduct of inquiry, and in particular means that knowledge is more than correct information as such.

The Security/Definiteness Trade-off and the Contrast Between Science and Common Sense

It is a basic principle of epistemology that increased confidence in the correctness of our estimates can always be secured at the price of decreased accuracy. For in general *an inverse relationship obtains between the definiteness or precision of our information and its substantiation: detail and security stand in a competing relationship.* We estimate the height of the tree at *around* 25 feet. We are *quite sure* that the tree is 25 ± 5 feet high. We are *virtually certain* that its height is 25 ± 10 feet. But we can be *completely and absolutely sure* that its height is between 1 inch and 100 yards. Of this we are "completely sure" in the sense that we are "absolutely certain," "certain beyond the shadow of a doubt," "as certain as we can be of anything in the world," "so sure that I would be willing to stake my life on it," and the like. For any sort of estimate whatsoever

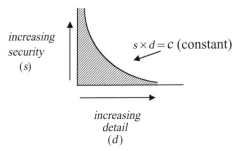

DISPLAY 1.1. Duhem's Law: the complementarity trade-off between security and definiteness in estimation. *Note:* The shaded region inside the curve represents the parametric range of achievable information, with the curve indicating the limit of what is realizable. The concurrent achievement of great detail *and* security is impracticable.

there is always a characteristic trade-off relationship between the evidential *security* of the estimate, on the one hand (as determinable on the basis of its probability or degree of acceptability), and on the other hand its contentual *detail* (definiteness, exactness, precision, etc.).

And so a complementarity relationship of the sort depicted in Display 1.1 obtains. This was adumbrated in the ideas of the French physicist Pierre Maurice Duhem (1861–1916) and may accordingly be called "Duhem's Law."[1] In his classic work on the aim and structure of physical theory,[2] Duhem wrote as follows:

A law of physics possesses a certainty much less immediate and much more difficult to estimate than a law of common sense, but it surpasses the latter by

[1] It is both common and convenient in matters of learning and science to treat ideas and principles eponymously. An eponym, however, is a person *for* whom something is named, and not necessarily *after* whom this is done, seeing that eponyms can certainly be honorific as well as genetic. Here at any rate eponyms are sometimes used to make the point that the work of the person at issue has *suggested* rather than *originated* the idea or principle at issue.

[2] *La théorie physique: son objet, et sa structure* (Paris: Chevalier and Rivière, 1906); tr. by Philip P. Wiener, *The Aim and Structure of Physical Theory* (Princeton: Princeton University Press, 1954). This principle did not elude Neils Bohr himself, the father of complementarity theory in physics: "In later years Bohr emphasized the importance of complementarity for matters far removed from physics. There is a story that Bohr was once asked in German what is the quality that is complementary to truth (*Wahrheit*). After some thought he answered clarity (*Klarheit*)." Steven Weinberg, *Dreams of a Final Theory* (New York: Pantheon Books, 1992), p. 74 footnote 10.

the minute and detailed precision of its predictions. . . . The laws of physics can acquire this minuteness of detail only by sacrificing something of the fixed and absolute certainty of common-sense laws. *There is a sort of teeter-totter of balance between precision and certainty: one cannot be increased except to the detriment of the other.*[3]

In effect, these two factors – security and detail – stand in a relation of inverse proportionality, as shown in the picture of Display 1.1.

Note that the relationship at issue envisions the boundary of realizable information as set by a curve of the form $x \times y = c$, or equivalently $y = c/x$. Accordingly, the sum total of the area of accessibility lying under this curve is given by $\int y\,dx = c \int dx/x \approx \log x$. On this basis the overall size of the body of high-quality information that combines security and definiteness to an acceptable extent is given by a logarithmic measure. It will be useful to bear this in mind as the discussion proceeds.

Science versus Common Sense

Duhem emphasized that this relationship has important implications for the standing of the exact sciences where, after all, we always aim at the maximum of achievable universality, precision, and exactness. Thus in physics when we make the assertion, "The melting point of lead is 327.7 degrees Celsius," we are claiming that *all* pieces of (pure) lead will *unfailingly* melt at *exactly* this temperature. We certainly do not mean to assert that most pieces of (pure) lead will *probably* melt at *somewhere around* this temperature. (And in this regard, there would be a potential problem, should it turn out, for example, that there is no melting point at all and that what is actually at issue is the center of a statistical distribution.) In aspiration always and in practice generally, the theoretical claims of science involve no hedging, no fuzziness, no incompleteness, and no exceptions; they are strict: precise, wholly explicit, exceptionless, and unshaded. Here we operate at the lower right-hand side of the Display 1.1 curve.

After all, in intent and in aspiration science aims to characterize nature as it really is. And since (as we certainly believe) nature is fully definite and detailed, science endeavors to infuse these characteristics

---

[3] Duhem, *La théorie physique*, pp. 178–79. Italics supplied.

into the claims it stakes regarding the world. It scorns the very idea of claiming that matters stand roughly thus-wise or that things function something like such-and-such. Unlike everyday-life communication, the exact sciences stand committed not just to truth but to accuracy and exactness as well. And this, their seeming strength, is their Achilles' heel as well.

By contrast, the situation of ordinary life is very different; when we assert that "peaches are delicious" we are maintaining something like "most people will find the eating of suitably grown and duly matured peaches a rather pleasurable experience." Such a statement has all sorts of built-in safeguards on the order of "more or less," "in ordinary circumstances," "by and large," "normally," "when all things are equal," "rather plausible," and so on. They are not really laws in the usual sense, but rules of thumb, a matter of practical lore rather than scientific rigor. But this enables them to achieve great security. For there is safety in vagueness: a factual claim can always acquire security through inexactness. Take "there are rocks in the world" or "dogs can bark." It is virtually absurd to characterize such everyday life contentions as fallible: their security lies in their very indefiniteness and imprecision.

And there is good reason for adopting this resort to vagueness in everyday life, for protecting our claims to reliability and trustworthiness becomes crucial in personal interactions. We proceed in cognitive matters in much the same way that lenders such as banks proceed in financial matters. We extend credit to others, doing so at first to only a relatively modest extent. When and if they comport themselves in a manner that shows that this credit was well deserved and warranted, we proceed to give them more credit and extend their credit limit. By responding to trust in a responsible way, one improves one's credit rating in cognitive contexts much as in financial contexts. The same sort of mechanism is at work on both sides of the analogy: creditworthy comportment engenders a reputation on which further credit can be based; earned credit is like money in the bank, well worth the measure needed for its maintenance and for preserving the good name that is now at stake. Thus we constantly rely on experts in a plethora of situations, continually placing reliance on doctors, lawyers, architects, and other professionals. But they, too, must so perform as to establish credit, not just as individuals but, even more crucially, for their profession as a whole.[4] And much the same sort of thing holds for other sources of information. (The example of our senses is a particularly important case in point.) In everyday life, in sum, we prioritize correctness over accuracy.

However, while everyday-life common sense trades definiteness for security, science does the very reverse, with the result that its claims become subject to greater insecurity. As Duhem put it:

> A law of physics is always provisional and relative. It is provisional also in that it does not connect realities but symbols, and that is because there are always cases where the symbol no longer corresponds to reality; the laws of physics cannot be maintained except by continual retouching and modification. . . . One might be tempted to draw the strange conclusion that the knowledge of the laws of physics constitutes a degree of knowledge inferior to the simple knowledge of the laws of common sense.

Science decidedly prioritizes accuracy and detail over security. So as Duhem himself maintained, his principle both characterizes and explains the profound differences between the nature of our knowledge in science and in the matters of everyday life.

Further Ramifications

Duhem's Law of Security/Detail Complementarity has substantial implications for the modus operandi of inquiry. Thus one of its fundamental implications is represented by the following observation:

THESIS 1: *Insofar as our thinking is vague, truth is accessible even in the face of error.*

Consider the situation in which you correctly accept *P*-or-*Q*. But – so let it be supposed – the truth of this disjunction is entirely rooted in *P*, while *Q* is flatly false. However, you accept *P*-or-*Q* only because you are mistakenly convinced of the truth of *Q*, while it so happens that *P* is something you actually disbelieve. Nevertheless, despite your error, your belief is entirely true.[5] Consider a concrete instance. You

---

4 Compare H. M. Vollmer and D. L. Mills, eds., *Professionalization* (Englewood Cliffs, NJ: Prentice Hall, 1966). This credit, once earned, is generally safeguarded and maintained by institutional means: licensing procedures, training qualifications, professional societies, codes of professional practice, and the like.
5 Examples of this sort indicate why philosophers are unwilling to identify *knowledge* with *true belief*, even where belief is justified.

believe that Smith bought some furniture because he bought a table. However it was, in fact, a chair that he bought, something you would flatly reject because you believe he bought a table. All the same, your belief that he bought some furniture is unquestionably correct. The error in which you are involved, although very real, is yet not so grave as to destabilize the truth of your belief.

Ignorance is a matter of inability to answer questions properly. But one has to be careful in this regard. Answering a question informatively is not just a matter of providing a *correct* answer but also a matter of offering an *exact* answer. Thus consider the question "What is the population of Shanghai?" If I respond "More than ten and less than ten billion" I have provided a *correct* answer, albeit one that is not particularly helpful.

So the irony of it is that insofar as our ignorance of relevant matters leads us to be vague in our judgments, we nevertheless may well manage to enhance the likelihood of being right. The fact of the matter is that we have this:

THESIS 2: *By constraining us to make vaguer judgments, ignorance enhances our access to correct information (albeit at the cost of less detail and precision).*

For example, if I have forgotten that Seattle is in Washington State, then if "forced to guess" I might well erroneously locate it in Oregon. Nevertheless, my vague judgment that "Seattle is located in the Northwestern United States" is quite correct.

This state of affairs means that when the truth of our claims is critical we generally "play it safe" and make our commitments less definite and detailed. And in practical matters in particular, such rough guidance is often altogether enough. We need not know precisely how much rain there will be to make it sensible for us to take an umbrella. Nevertheless in those matters where exactness counts this pathway to truth is rather problematic.

Knowledge in Perspective

Duhem's Law of Cognitive Complementarity means that it is going to be a fact of life in the general theory of estimation that the harder we push for certainty – for security of our claims – the vaguer we will have to make these claims and the more general and imprecise they will become. And so if we want our scientific claims to have realistic import – taking them to provide an account of how matters actually stand – we have to reconstrue them loosely. Take the atomic theory. We should not – cannot – say that atoms are in every detail as the science of the day holds them to be: that the "Atomic Theory" section of our *Handbook of Physics* succeeds in every jot and tittle in characterizing reality as it actually is. But if we "fuzz things up" – if we claim merely that physical reality is granular and that atoms exist and have roughly such-and-such features – then what we say is no longer subject to (reasonable) doubt.

The complementarity of security and detail accordingly carries important lessons for the realization of knowledge. For one thing, seeing that informativeness is a pivotal factor here, it means that knowledge calls for more than mere correctness. And, for another, it means that knowledge is something difficult, something we do not achieve all that easily. For on its basis, knowledge qualifies as such not only through its claims to truth but also through its informativeness. The fact that quality is going to be a key factor here means that the quantity of information cannot be equated with the quantity of knowledge.

In the pursuit of knowledge we seek and demand more than the mere truth about things. For truth comes to us too cheap and easy when it is secured at the price of uninformativeness. Knowledge does not issue from trivial truth, it must contribute to our understanding of things. And so, both security and informativeness figure among the essentials for knowledge. But it lies in the nature of our human situation as finite inquiring beings that only so much can be accomplished along these lines. Duhem's cognitive complementarity law constrains us to make choices: we cannot "have it both ways." And just these considerations lead to a question that will set the theme for the rest of the book: Just what are the ramifications and implications that such limits pose for the development of knowledge?

2

Kant's Conception of Knowledge as Systematized Information

(1) Knowledge is not just a matter of information as such, but of information that is coherently and cohesively systematized. (2) This view of knowledge as properly systematized information – in effect, information as structured in an idealized expository treatise – goes back to Immanuel Kant. (3) Cognitive systematization is hierarchical in structure because a systemic organization of the exposition of the information at issue into successively subordinate units becomes paramount here. And, viewed in this light, structure will of course reflect significance with larger units dominating over subordinate ones.

Distinguishing Knowledge and Information

The interplay between knowledge and information is pivotal for the present deliberations. Actual information (in contrast with misinformation) requires little more than truth. But *knowledge* is something far more demanding: it calls for information that is organized, purified, systematized. It makes no sense to say "It is known that *p*, but it may possibly not be so (or . . . "there are considerations that lead to doubt about it")." From the cognitive point of view, knowledge is money in the bank. It must fit together coherently. The very concept of knowledge is such that what is known must be systemically consolidated: the matter of quality will also play a crucial role. For items of information are not created equal. Some are minute and trivial, others large and portentous. So there is little point to merely doing a nose count here. Only information that is scrutinized, verified, coordinated, and systematized can plausibly qualify to be regarded as knowledge. Whatever else it is, knowledge is information of substantial quality. And this leads to the question: How is knowledge related to information in strictly quantitative terms?

Since factual contentions are formulated symbolically, the quantitative assessment of raw information can be made by measuring expository text – that is, by looking to the amount of text expended in stating the matter. Information can thus be assessed – in a first approximation at least – in terms of sheer textuality, subject to the idea that the ampler and fuller its exposition, the more information this text account conveys.

Knowledge, on the other hand, is something very different, and mere information – unreconstructed textuality – does not do what is needed there. For knowledge does not consist in information as such but only in appropriately systematized information. And accordingly, knowledge is not a matter of the extent of text actually devoted to the issue, but rather requires an assessment of systemic enmeshment. To view knowledge in textual terms would require a radically different approach, one that looks not merely to sheer quantity of text but rather to the textual role of the information at issue.

But just how is this idea of knowledge and its systematization to be implemented?

Kant on the Systematicity of Knowledge

In the eighteenth century Immanuel Kant (1724–1804) had eloquently argued that the mission of rational inquiry is the systemic organization of knowledge: its coordination into one coherent structure under the guiding aegis of unifying principles.

If we consider in its whole range the knowledge obtained for us by the understanding, we find that what is peculiarly distinctive of reason in its attitude to this body of knowledge, is that it prescribes and seeks to achieve its *systematization*, that is, to exhibit the connection of its parts in conformity with a single principle. . . . This unity of reason always presupposes an idea, (or plan), namely, that of the form of a whole of knowledge – a whole which is prior to the determinate knowledge of the parts and which contains the conditions that determine *a priori* for every part its position and relation to the other parts. . . . This idea accordingly demands a complete [organic] unity in the knowledge obtained by understanding by which this knowledge is to be not a mere contingent aggregate, but a system connected according to nec-essary laws. We may not say that this idea is a concept of the object, but only of the thoroughgoing unity of such concepts, in so far as that unity serves as a rule for the understanding. These concepts or reason are not derived from nature; on the contrary, we interrogate nature in accordance with these ideas, and consider our knowledge as defective so long as it is not adequate to them.   (*Critique of Pure Reason*, A645 = B673)

The paradigm of system that lay before Kant's eyes was that of sci-ence – of Euclid's systematization of Geometry, Archimedes' system-atization of statics, and Newton's systematization of celestial mechan-ics. And his model of rational systematization was that exemplified in the work of the great seventeenth-century rationalist philosophers: Descartes, Spinoza, and also Leibniz as expounded by the subsequent members of his school, especially Christian Wolff.[1]

As Kant saw it, adequate understanding can be achieved only through the systemic interrelating of facts. The mission of human reason is to furnish a basis for the rational comprehension of what we know and this can be accomplished only by positioning these facts as integral parts of an organic whole. Kant developed his biological analogy of system in the following terms:

[O]nly after we have spent much time in the collection of materials in some-what random fashion at the suggestion of an idea lying hidden in our minds, and after we have, indeed, over a long period assembled the materials in a merely technical manner, does it first become possible for us to discern the idea in a clearer light, and to devise a whole architectonically in accordance with the ends of reason. Systems seem to be formed in the manner of lowly organisms, through a *generatio aequivoca* from the mere confluence of assem-bled concepts, at first imperfect, and only gradually attaining to completeness, although they one and all have had their schema, as a original germ, in the sheer self-development of reason. Hence, not only is each system articulated in accordance with an idea, but they are one and all organically united in a system of human knowledge, as members of one whole.

(*Critique of Pure Reason*, A834 = B862)

---

[1] Leibniz's theory of cognitive systematization is detailed in the author's essay entitled "Leibniz and the Concept of a System" in his *Leibniz's Philosophy of Nature* (Dordrecht: D. Reidel, 1981), pp. 29–41. On the broader issues see the author's *Cognitive System-atization* (Oxford: Basil Blackwell, 1979).

The nature of systematization was accordingly explained by Kant along the lines of a fundamentally biological analogy:

In accordance with reason's legislative prescriptions, our diverse modes of knowledge must not be permitted to be a mere rhapsody, but must form a system. Only so can they further the essential ends of reason. By a system I understand the unity of the manifold modes of knowledge under one idea. This idea is the concept, provided by reason, of the form of a whole . . . [which] determines *a priori* not only the scope of its manifold content, but also the positions which the parts occupy relatively to one another. The scientific concept of reason contains, therefore, the end and the form of that whole which is congruent with this requirement. The unity of the end to which all the parts relate and in the idea of which they all stand in relation to one another, makes it possible for us to determine from our knowledge of the other parts whether any part be missing, and to prevent any arbitrary addition, or in respect of its completeness [to discover] any indeterminateness that does not conform to the limits which are thus determined *a priori*. The whole is thus an organised unity (*articulatio*), and not an aggregate (*coacervatio*). It may grow from within (*per intussusceptionem*), but not by external addition (*per appositionem*). It is thus like an animal body.   (*Critique of Pure Reason*, A832–3 = B860–61)

In reasoning along these lines, Kant put us on the right tack regarding the nature of cognitive systematization. Here completeness and comprehensiveness become paramount desiderata, and a body of information constitutes systemic knowledge when its articulation is characterized by such organic unity. Thus as Kant sensibly saw it, only a body of information coherently systematized on principles of organic interlinkage can be regarded as constituting knowledge. Authentic knowledge must form part of a coherently integrated system, and every part of such a system must serve in the role of a contributory sub-system: an organ of the overall organism. And so, despite various historical anticipations, this idea – that to qualify as authentic, cognitively significant *knowledge*, informative contentions must be part of a system – deserves to be called Kant's Principle of Cognitive Systematicity thanks to the prominence and centrality that he gave to this idea in insisting that knowledge, in its qualitative and honorific sense, is a matter of the extent to which information is coherently systematized.

10 chapters per book
10 sections per chapter
10 paragraphs per section
10 sentences per paragraph
10 words per sentence

DISPLAY 2.1. A Hypothetical Treatise.

The Hierarchical Textualization of Knowledge

Kant's line of thought can be carried a step further to the idea that in a well-designed systemic exposition of information, *systemic role mirrors cognitive status*. In a deductive systematization such as that of Euclid, the axioms have priority over the theorems.[2] Here the order of exposition reflects cognitive fundamentality and thereby dominance. However, in a more discursive exposition it is not so much order as structure that is determinative. Some ideas are chapter correlative and require substantial development; others deserve a mere section – or paragraph or sentence. Dominance of hierarchical placement in an analytical table of contents reflects cognitive status showing that length and detail of treatment come into correlation.

Now in the ideal case, the cognitive significance of themes and topics can be assessed via the organizational status dedicated to their treatment. And so the systemic structure of a book's discussion domain in terms of its constituent elites could be mapped out by dividing it into successive units as per the hypothetical treatise of Display 2.1. And this in turn intends a systemic structure with layers of components at different hierarchical levels as per Display 2.2 (which for simplicity depicts the situation based on 3 rather than 10).

In this light, the hierarchical exposition of information through its exfoliation into successively subordinate units becomes paramount for the quantitative assessment of knowledge. Some items of information represent important ideas that are chapter-worthy; others are

[2] Kant had in view not only Euclid's *Elements* and Newton's *Principia* but also the philosophical systematizations of the scholastic and neo-scholastic eras of Aquinas, Scotus, Suarez and Wolff. For further details on these matters see the author's *Cognitive Systematization* (Oxford: Basil Blackwell, 1979).

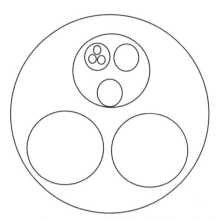

DISPLAY 2.2. The systemic structure of a domain via units of successive expository subordination.

smaller scale, worthy of a sentence – or a paragraph at most. And this sort of thing would (ideally) be reflected in the taxonomic depth of an analytically well-designed table of contents. And, of course, this book analogy could be replicated on a larger scale in such a sequence as cognitive domain, discipline, substantive, specialty, problem-area, problem, problem-component.

What we have here is a picture of nested aggregation with findings at a given level of quality in systemic significance encompassing a multitude of others at lower levels of quality. Quantity and quality are thus brought into correlation. In an appropriately structured exposition, the table of content status of ideas and theses is bound to reflect their cognitive importance.

But just how does such an hierarchical expository architectonic develop as we elaborate a cognitive system by pressing our efforts ever further in the course of rational inquiry?

3

Spencer's Law of Cognitive Development

(1) Herbert Spencer's "Law of Cognitive Development" through taxonomic exfoliation depicts an important phenomenon in the growth of cognition. (2) This is amply illustrated by the history of science, which tells an ongoing story of taxonomic complexification. (3) Such increasing complexity is the price exacted by scientific progress. (4) On the basis of Spencer's Law it can be seen that the actual knowledge inherent in the mass of information stands not as the volume thereof, but merely as its logarithm.

Spencer's Law: the Dynamics of Cognitive Complexity

Already well before Darwin, the English philosopher Herbert Spencer (1820–1903) argued that organic evolution is characterized by Karl Ernst von Baer's (1792–1876) law of development "from the homogeneous to the heterogeneous" and thereby produces an ever-increasing elaborateness of detail and complexity of articulation.[1] As Spencer saw it, organic species in the course of their development confront a successive series of environmental obstacles, and with each successful turning along the maze of developmental challenges the organism becomes selectively more highly specialized in its bio-design, and thereby more tightly attuned to the particular features of its ecological context.[2]

---

[1] Herbert Spencer, *First Principles*, 7th ed. (London: Appleton's, 1889); see sect. 14–17 of Part II, "The Law of Evolution."

[2] On the process in general see John H. Holland, *Hidden Order: How Adaptation Builds Complexity* (Reading, MA: Addison Wesley, 1995). Regarding the specifically

Now this view of the developmental process may be of limited applicability in *biological* evolution, but there can be little question about its holding good in *cognitive* evolution. For rational beings will of course try simple things first and thereafter be led step by step toward an ever-enhanced complexification. In the course of rational inquiry we try the simple solutions first, and only thereafter, if and when they cease to work – when they are ruled out by further developments – do we move on to the more complex. Matters go along smoothly until an oversimple solution becomes destabilized by enlarged experience. For a time we get by with the comparatively simpler options – until the expanding information about the world's *modus operandi* made possible by enhanced new means of observation and experimentation insists otherwise. And with the expansion of knowledge those new accessions make ever-increasing demands.

And this state of affairs means that the course of empirical inquiry moves historically in the direction of ever-increasing complexity. The developmental tendency of our intellectual enterprises – natural science preeminent among them – is generally in the direction of greater complication and sophistication. In this way, cognitive evolution in its various forms – whether of animal species or of literary genres – ongoingly confronts us with products of greater and greater complexity.[3]

In scientific inquiry, in particular, we look to the most economical theory accommodation for the amplest body of currently available experience. Induction – here short for "the scientific method" in general – proceeds by constructing the most straightforward and economical structures able to house the available data comfortably while yet affording answers to our questions.[4] Accordingly, economy and simplicity serve as cardinal directives for inductive reasoning, whose procedure is that of the precept: "Resolve your cognitive problems in the simplest, most economical way that is compatible with

evolutionary aspect of the process see Robert N. Brandon, *Adaptation and Environment* (Princeton: Princeton University Press, 1990).

[3] On the issues of this paragraph compare Stuart Kaufmann, *At Home in the Universe: To Search for the Laws of Self-Organization and Complexity* (New York: Oxford University Press, 1995).

[4] For further details see the author's *Induction* (Oxford: Basil Blackwell, 1980).

a sensible exploitation of the information at your disposal." But we always encounter limits here. Simple solutions take us only so far.

An inner tropism toward increasing complexity is thus built into the very nature of the scientific project as we have it. And this circumstance leads to what may be called Spencer's Law of Cognitive Development:

> As a body of information on any given topic grows in size the complexity of that body – its inner variation and diversification – also increases.

What we have here is a thesis to the effect that cognitive progress is accompanied by and can be measured in terms of the taxonomic complexity of the information manifold at hand.

Our cognitive efforts manifest a Manichaean-style struggle between complexity and simplicity – between the impetus to comprehensiveness (amplitude) and the impetus to system (economy). We want our theories to be as extensive and all-encompassing as possible and at the same time to be elegant and economical. The first desideratum pulls in one direction, the second in the other. And the accommodation reached here is never actually stable. As our experience expands in the quest for greater adequacy and comprehensiveness, the old theory structures become destabilized – the old theories no longer fit the full range of available fact. And so the theoretician goes back to the old drawing board. What he comes up with here is – and in the circumstances must be – something more elaborate, more *complex* than what was able to do the job before those new complications arose (though we do, of course, sometimes achieve local simplifications within an overall global complexification). We make do with the simple, but only up to the point when the demands of adequacy force additional complications upon us. Be it in cognitive or in practical matters, the processes and resources of yesteryear are rarely, if ever, up to the demands of the present. In consequence, the life-environment we create for ourselves grows increasingly complex. The Ockham's Razor injunction, "Never introduce complications unless and until you actually require them," accordingly represents a defining principle of practical reason that is at work within the cognitive project as well. And because we try the simplest solutions first, making them do until circumstances force us to do otherwise, it transpires that in the development of knowledge – as elsewhere in the domain of human artifice – progress is always a matter of complexification. In fact inherent impetus toward greater complexity pervades the entire realm of human creative effort. We find it in art; we find it in technology; and we certainly find it in the cognitive domain as well.[5]

How Cognitive Taxonomy Has Grown More Complex

It is instructive to examine somewhat more closely the role of complexity in the domain of cognition, now focusing on science in particular. Progress in natural science is a matter of dialogue or debate in a reciprocal interaction between theoreticians and experimentalists. The experimentalists probe nature to discern its reactions, to seek out phenomena. And the theoreticians take the resultant data and weave about them a fabric of hypotheses that is able to resolve our questions. Seeking to devise a framework of rational understanding, they construct their explanatory models to accommodate the findings that the experimentalists put at their disposal. Thereafter, once the theoreticians have had their say, the ball returns to the experimentalists' court. Employing new, more powerful means for probing nature, they bring new phenomena to view, new data for accommodation. Precisely because these data are new and inherently unpredictable on the basis of earlier knowledge, they often fail to fit the old theories. Theory extrapolations from the old data could not encompass them; the old theories do not accommodate them. A disequilibrium thus arises between available theory and novel data, and at this stage, the ball reenters the theoreticians' court. New theories must be devised to accommodate the new, nonconforming data. Accordingly, the theoreticians set about weaving a new theoretical structure into which the new data will fit. They endeavor to restore the equilibrium between theory and data once more. And when they succeed, the ball returns to the experimentalists' court, and the whole process starts over again.

---

[5] An interesting illustration of the extent to which lessons in the school of bitter experience have accustomed us to expect complexity is provided by the contrast between the pairs: rudimentary/nuanced; unsophisticated/sophisticated; plain/elaborate; simple/intricate. Note that in each case the second, complexity-reflective alternative has a distinctly more positive (or less negative) connotation than its opposite counterpart.

With the enhancement of investigative technology, the "window" looking out on nature's parametric space becomes constantly enlarged. Scientific theory formation is, in general, a matter of spotting a local regularity of phenomena in parametric space and then projecting it "across the board," maintaining it globally. But the theoretical claims of science are themselves never small-scale and local. They stipulate – quite ambitiously – how things are always and everywhere. In developing natural science we use the window of technological capability to scrutinize parametric space, continually augmenting our database and then generalizing on what we see. But what we have here is not a lunar landscape where once we have seen one sector we have seen it all, and where theory-projections from lesser data generally remain in place when further data come our way. Instead it does not require a sophisticated knowledge of history of science to realize that our worst fears are usually realized – that our theories seldom if ever survive intact in the wake of substantial extensions in our cognitive access to new sectors of nature's parametric space.

The history of science is a sequence of episodes of leaping to the wrong conclusions because new observational findings indicate matters are not quite so simple as heretofore thought. As ample experience indicates, our ideas about nature are subject to constant stresses – often radical and change-demanding – as we "explore" parametric space more extensively. The technologically mediated entry into new regions of parameter space constantly destabilizes the attained equilibrium between data and theory. Physical nature exhibits a very different aspect when viewed from the vantage point of different levels of sophistication in the technology of nature-investigator interaction. The possibility of change is ever-present. The ongoing destabilization of scientific theories is the price we pay for operating a simplicity-geared cognitive methodology in an actually complex world. The natural dialectic of scientific inquiry ongoingly impels us into ever-deeper levels of sophistication.[6]

---

[6] On the structure of dialectical reasoning see the author's *Dialectics* (Albany: State University of New York Press, 1977), and for the analogous role of such reasoning in philosophy see *The Strife of Systems* (Pittsburgh: University of Pittsburgh Press, 1985).

And in this context it is important to recognize that *growth in the taxonomical structure of science* is an integral part of the progress of science itself.[7] As the French physicist Pierre Auger has written:

At the time of Auguste Comte, the sciences could be classified in six of seven main categories known as disciplines, ranging from mathematics to sociology. Since then, during the nineteenth century and at the beginning of the twentieth, there has been what might be described as an intro-disciplinary dismemberment, each of the main categories splitting up into increasingly specialized fields, each of which rapidly assumed comparable importance to that of the actual disciplines from which it sprang. Chemistry, for example, in the days of Lavoisier formed a reasonably homogeneous entity, but chemists were soon obliged to choose between inorganic and organic chemistry; within the latter, a distinction arose during the second half of the nineteenth century between the chemistry of aromatic compounds and that of aliphatic compounds, the latter shortly being further subdivided into the study of saturated compounds and that of unsaturated compounds. Finally, at the present time, a chemist can devote a most useful research career entirely to a single chemical family. The same process can be discerned in physics and in biology.[8]

In the days of St. Thomas Aquinas, the whole of learning consisted of five or six areas, each of which had five or six sub-fields.[9] The history of science is an endlessly repetitive story of simple theories giving way to more complicated and sophisticated ones. The Greeks had four elements; in the nineteenth century Mendeleev had some sixty; by the 1900s this had gone to eighty, and nowadays we have a vast series of elemental stability states. Aristotle's cosmos had only spheres; Ptolemy's added epicycles; ours has a virtually endless proliferation of complex orbits that only supercomputers can approximate. Greek

---

[7] The scientific study of the taxonomy and morphology of science itself is a virtually nonexistent enterprise. Philosophers used to deal with these matters, but they abandoned them after the late 19th century, when science began to change too fast for those concerned to look at truth *sub specie aeternitatis*. (A good survey of the historical situation is given in Robert Flint, *Philosophy as Scientia Scientiarum: A History of Classifications of the Sciences* [Edinburgh and London: W. Blackwood and Sons, 1904].) In more recent days the subject has been left to bibliographers. For the older, "classical" attempts see Ernest Cushing Richardson, *Classification: Theoretical and Practical*, 3rd ed. (New York: H. W. Wilson, 1930).

[8] Pierre Auger, *Current Trends in Scientific Research* (Paris: UNESCO Publications, 1961), pp. 15–16.

[9] See Joseph Mariétan on *Problème de la classification des sciences d'Aristote à St. Thomas* (St. Maurice: Fribourg, 1901).

science was contained on a single shelf of books; that of the Newtonian age required a roomful; ours requires vast storage structures filled not only with books and journals but with photographs, tapes, floppy disks, and so on. Of the quantities currently recognized as the fundamental constants of physics, only one was contemplated in Newton's physics: the universal gravitational constant. A second was added in the nineteenth century, Avogadro's constant. The remaining six are all creatures of twentieth-century physics: the speed of light (the velocity of electromagnetic radiation in free space), the elementary charge, the rest mass of the electron, the rest mass of the proton, Planck's constant, and Boltzmann's constant.[10]

It would be naive – and quite wrong – to think that the course of scientific progress is one of increasing simplicity. The very reverse is the case: scientific progress is a matter of complexification because over-simple theories invariably prove untenable in a complex world. Our ever-more-sophisticated searches invariably engender changes of mind, thereby moving us in the direction of an ever-more-complex and sophisticated picture of the world. In this regard our commitment to simplicity and systematicity, though methodologically necessary, is ontologically unavailing, for our methodological commitment to simplicity should not and does not preclude the substantive discovery of complexity.

This complexification of scientific knowledge is also manifested vividly in the fact that our cognitive taxonomies are bursting at the seams. Consider the example of taxonomic structure of physics. We may assume a three-layer taxonomy: the field as a whole, the branches thereof, and the sub-branches of the branches. The taxonomic situation prevailing toward the beginning of this century is pictured in Display 3.1. It is interesting to contrast this picture of the taxonomic situation in physics with the picture of the situation in subsequent decades as given in Display 3.2.

These tables tell a significant story. In the 11th (1911) edition of the *Encyclopedia Britannica*, physics is described as a discipline composed of 9 constituent branches (e.g., "Acoustics" or "Electricity and Magnetism"), which were themselves partitioned into 15 further specialties

---

[10] See B. W. Petley, *The Fundamental Physical Constants and the Frontiers of Measurement* (Bristol: Hilger, 1985).

Astronomy
   —Astrophysics
   —Celestial Mechanics
Acoustics
Optics
   —Theoretical Optics
   —Spectroscopy
Mechanics
Heat
   —Calorimetry
   —Theory of Radiation
   —Thermodynamics
   —Thermometry
Electricity and Magnetism
   —Electrochemistry
   —Electrokinetics
   —Electrometallurgy
   —Electrostatics
   —Thermoelectricity
   —Diamagnetism
   —Electromagnetism
Pneumatics
Energetics
Instrumentation

DISPLAY 3.1. The taxonomy of physics in the 11th edition of the *Encyclopedia Britannica* (1911). *Note*: Adapted from the Classified List of Articles at the end of Vol. XXIX (index volume).

(e.g., "Thermoelectricity" and "Celestial Mechanics"). The 15th (1974) version of the *Britannica* divides physics into 12 branches whose sub-fields are – seemingly – too numerous for listing. (However the 14th, 1960s edition carried a special article entitled "Physics, Articles on," which surveyed more than 130 special topics in the field.) When the National Science Foundation launched its inventory of physical specialties with the National Register of Scientific and Technical Personnel in 1954, it divided physics into 12 areas with 90 specialties. By 1970 these figures had increased to 16 and 210, respectively. And the process continues unabated to the point that people are increasingly reluctant to embark on this classifying project at all.

In the nineteenth century, a different situation prevailed. Then, all of the great figures of the philosophy of science of this era – Comte, Whewell, Mill, Spencer, Peirce – made substantial examinations of the

1954	1970
Astronomy (16 specialties)	Astronomy
Acoustics (7 specialties)	—Solar-Planetary Relationships
Optics (8 specialties)	(9 specialties)
Mechanics and Heat (13 specialties)	—Planetology (6 specialties)
Electromagnetism (6 specialties)	—11 Further Astrophysical
Solid State (8 specialties)	Specialties
Atomic and Molecular Physics	Acoustics (9 specialties)
(5 specialties)	Optics (10 specialties)
Nuclear Physics (9 specialties)	Mechanics (10 specialties)
Theoretical Physics: Quantum Physics	Thermal Physics (9 specialties)
(4 specialties) (= Elementary	Electromagnetism (8 specialties)
Particles and Fields)	Solids (25 specialties)
Theoretical Physics: Classical	Fluids (9 specialties)
(3 specialties)	Atmospheric Structure and Dynamics
Electronics (7 specialties)	(16 specialties)
Instrumentation and Miscellaneous	Atoms and Molecules (10 specialties)
(4 specialties)	Nuclei (3 specialties)
	Elementary Particles and Fields
	(6 specialties)
	Physical Chemistry (25 specialties)
	Biophysics (6 specialties)
	Solid Earth Geographics (10 specialties)
	Instrumentation (28 specialties)

DISPLAY 3.2. Physics specialties in the "National Register of Scientific and Technical Personnel" for 1954 and 1970. Data from *American Science Manpower: 1954–1956* (Washington, DC: National Science Foundation Publications, 1961) and "Specialties List for Use with 1970 National Register of Scientific and Technical Personnel" (Washington, DC: National Science Foundation Publications, 1970).

systematic structure of science as a whole, including the inventory and arrangement of its component branches and subdivisions.[11]

The rapid expansion of interest in the taxonomy of knowledge during the nineteenth century (in the wake of the growth of historical

---

[11] The better older surveys of the historical situation are Julius Pelzholdt, *Bibliotheca Bibliographica* (Leipzig: W. Engelmann, 1866). Charles W. Shields, *Philosophia Ultima*, vol. II, *The History of the Sciences and the Logic of the Sciences or the Science of the Sciences* (New York: Scribner's, 1888–1905), 3. vols; Robert Flint, *Philosophy as Scientia Scientiarum and History of the Classification of the Sciences* (Edinburgh and London: Blackwood, 1904); and Ernest C. Richardson, *Classification: Theoretical and Practical*, 3rd ed. (New York: H.W. Wilson, 1930).

interest) is a phenomenon as striking as its modern neglect. No major nineteenth-century philosopher of science failed to give extensive consideration to the problem of classifying the sciences, and no major twentieth-century philosopher of science has touched it.[12] Substantially the same story can be told for every field of science. The emergence of new disciplines, branches, and specialties is manifest everywhere. And as though to negate this tendency and maintain unity, one finds an ongoing evolution of interdisciplinary syntheses – physical chemistry, astrophysics, biochemistry, and so on. The very attempt to counteract fragmentation produces new fragments. Indeed, the phenomenology of this domain is nowadays so complex that some writers believe the idea of a "natural taxonomy of science" must be abandoned altogether.[13] The expansion of the scientific literature is so great that natural science has in recent years been disintegrating before our very eyes. An ever-larger number of ever-more refined specialties has made it increasingly difficult for experts in a given branch of science to achieve a thorough understanding about what is going on, even in the specialty next door.

Evolving Complexity

The ongoing refinement in the division of cognitive labor as the information explosion continues has resulted in a literal dis-integration of knowledge. The "progress of knowledge" has been marked by a proliferation of increasingly narrow specialties – and no single person can keep up with it. A person's understanding of matters outside his or her immediate bailiwick is bound to become superficial. No counting scientist now has a detailed understanding of his or her own field beyond the boundaries of a narrow subspecialty. At their home base scientists know the details, nearby they have an understanding of generalities, but at a greater remove they can be no more than informed amateurs.

The "unity of science" to which many theorists aspire may possibly come to be realized at the level of highly general concepts and theories

---

[12] For an analysis see R. G. A. Dolby, "Classification of the Sciences: The Nineteenth-Century Tradition" [unpublished study issued for its author by the University of Kent at Canterbury ca. 1975].

[13] See John Dupré, *The Disorder of Things: Metaphysical Foundations of the Disunity of Science* (Cambridge, MA: Harvard University Press, 1993).

shared between different sciences – that is, at the level of ideational overlaps. For as one acute observer has written:

But this very over-specialization has provoked an inverse or rather a comple-mentary process, that of interdisciplinary synthesis; thus, from physics and chemistry there has grown up a new discipline of physical chemistry, which is influenced by both these sciences. This process has given rise to a whole series of new sciences with double or even triple names-astrophysics, biochemistry, mathematical chemistry, physico-chemical biology, etc. Thus, the diverging lines of the subjects of scientific research are connected by cross-links which restore unity to the whole.[14]

All the same, for every conceptual commonality and shared element a dozen differentiations and distinctions will emerge.

The increasing complexity of our world picture is a striking phe-nomenon throughout the development of modern science. Whatever information the sciences achieve is bought dearly through the prolif-eration of complexity. It is, of course, possible that the development of physics may eventually carry us to theoretical unification where every-thing that we class among the "laws of nature" belongs to one grand unified theory – one all-encompassing deductive systematization inte-grated even more tightly than that Newton's *Principia Mathematica*.[15] But on all discernible indications the covers of this elegantly contrived "book of nature" will have to encompass a mass of ever more elaborate diversity and variety. And this integration, on the principle of a pyra-mid, will cover further down an endlessly expansive range of the most variegated components.

The lesson of such considerations is clear. In the course of scientific progress our knowledge grows not just in extent but also in complexity. The history of science tells an ongoing story of taxonomic complexifi-cation, and in modern science extensive specialization and division of labor continue inexorably. The years of apprenticeship that separate master from novice increase. A science that moves continually from an over-simple picture of the world to one that is more complex must have more elaborate processes for its effective cultivation. And as the

---

[14] Pierre Auger, *Current Trends in Scientific Research* (Paris: UNESCO Publications, 1961), pp. 15–16.
[15] See Steven Weinberg, *Dreams of a Final Theory* (New York: Pantheon, 1992). See also Edoardo Amaldi, "The Unity of Physics," *Physics Today*, 261 (September, 1973), p. 23–29. Compare also C. F. von Weizsäcker, "The Unity of Physics," in Ted Bastin (ed.), *Quantum Theory and Beyond* (Cambridge: Cambridge University Press, 1971).

scientific enterprise itself grows more extensive, the greater elaborateness of its productions requires an increasingly intricate intellectual
structure for its accommodation. The complexification of scientific
process and product escalate hand in hand. The regulative ideal of
science is to integrate our knowledge of the world's modus operandi
into a coherent and cohesive unifying system. But the world's complexity makes this an aspiration rather than an accomplished fact: it
represents a goal toward which we may be able to make progress but
which we will never attain.[16]

Yet complexity is not unqualified negative. It is an unavoidable con-
comitant of progress in this domain, for we could not extend our
cognitive or our practical grasp of the world without taking its complexification in stride. Throughout the realm of human artifice –
cognitive artifice included – further complexity is part and parcel
of extending the frontiers of progress. The struggle with complexity that we encounter throughout our cognitive efforts is an inherent
and unavoidable aspect of the human condition's progressive impetus
to doing more and doing it better.

Spencer's law of cognitive development through taxonomic complexification accordingly carries a mixed bag of news in its wake. The
good news is that cognitive progress through the enticement of information brings conceptual progress and thereby deeper understanding
in its wake. But the bad news is that this progress can be realized only at
great cost in regard both to its production and its utilization. For its production calls for even more information and thereby an ever-growing
investment of resources and of effort. Operating at the frontier of any
branch of natural science becomes increasingly more demanding and
difficult.[17]

A Quantitative Perspective

As we examine the cognitive complexity reflected in the heterogeneity
and diversification of relevant information, at what pace does it grow
as inquiry proceeds? Here it seems sensible to go back to basics.

---

[16] For variations on this theme see the author's *The Limits of Science* (Berkeley: University
of California Press, 1984).

[17] On further issues relevant to these ideas see also the author's *Scientific Progress*
(Oxford: Basil Blackwell, 1978).

Spencer's Law of Cognitive Development means in effect that the extent of our actual knowledge about the world and its ways will stand correlative with the complexity of its systemic articulation. Now complexity is not a feature of information as such but rather of its *structure*. And this structural complexity is indicated by and indeed encompassed in the taxonomy by whose means we organize this information. It is a matter of the distinctions and classifications we use in giving a coherent exposition of the body of information at issue. The systemic architecture of our information is the crux here.

And seeing that knowledge is a matter of organized and systematized information, informational complexity becomes our best standard for assessing the extent of its attainment. Knowledge grows in line with the extent to which our increasingly extensive and thereby complex body of information expands its hierarchial structure.

Returning to the text-geared themes of Chapter 2, let us consider the hierarchy of informational structure represented by the sequence: sentence, paragraph, section, chapter, volumes, shelf, cabinet, room, library, library system, and so on. Along just these lines, the hierarchical structure of a body of information comes into view. And it can now be assessed, in principle, along quantitative lines. For illustration, (and a simple example), let us hitch our wagon to the star of orders of magnitude and assume a factor of 10 all along the way: 10 sentences to be a paragraph, 10 paragraphs to a section, 10 sections to a chapter, and so on. Assuming a superlibrary of 100 million volumes (the Library of Congress nowadays has some 20 million) we contemplate the following hierarchy:

sentences	10,000,000,000
paragraphs	1,000,000,000
sections	100,000,000
chapters	10,000,000
volumes	1,000,000
shelves	100,000
cabinets	10,000
rooms	1,000
libraries	100
library complexes	10
library systems	1

Thus the hierarchic depth of body of our million volumes is 10, that is to say, log 10,000,000,000. And more generally, we can say that the hierarchic depth of a body of information can be measured by the logarithm of its textual volume.

Now on the basis of Spencer's Law we would expect that the cognitive sophistication that reflects actual knowledge would be faithfully reflected in the taxonomic complexity of the information at issue.

Spencer's Law is thus the pathway to determining the relation of knowledge to mere information, enabling us at the same time to quantify the assessment of knowledge. And on this basis, the complex and sophisticated information – the premium information that constitutes actual knowledge – will increase in proportion not with the mere bulk of our body of information as such, but only with its logarithm.

A look at the process of knowledge development indicates the plausibility of this perspective. By all indications, the taxonomy needed for the cognitive accommodation of a body of information (I) – and correspondingly the complexity of that information – grows in inverse proportion to the volume of that body of information ($\#I$); the larger a body of information already is, the more sedately its taxonomy expands. Accordingly we have the relation

$$\frac{d}{dI}\, compl\,(I) \approx \frac{1}{\#I}.$$

And on this basis we have

$$compl\,(I) \approx \int \frac{d\#I}{\#I} \propto \log\#I.$$

For on its basis the complexity of a body of information as reflected in its taxonomic depth stands not as its volume but merely as the logarithm thereof. This relationship gives a quantitative expression to Spencer's Law, that with the quantitative growth of information there indeed is a natural increase in heterogeneity (in taxonomic diversification) – albeit at a decelerating pace. With the expansion of information, its complexity does increase, but only at a decreasing (logarithmic) rate. And in this quantified form, Spencer's Law of Logarithmic Development has profound implications for the development of knowledge.

4

Gibbon's Law of Logarithmic Returns

(1) Cognitive progress is subject to Kant's Principle of Question propagation to the effect that new knowledge always brings new questions in its wake. (2) However, the increase of mere information does not yield a corresponding increase in knowledge: knowledge is not proportional to the volume of information, but only to its logarithm. This key epistemological principle traces back at least to Edward Gibbon. (3) Gibbon's Law of Logarithmic Returns as a principle of the realm of conception parallels the Weber-Fechner Law in the epistemics of perception. (4) The Law of Logarithmic Returns accounts for Max Planck's Thesis that scientific progress becomes ever more difficult, so that diminishing returns on effort are an unavoidable facet of inquiry.

Kant's Principle of Questions Propagation

New knowledge that emerges from the progress of inquiry can bear very differently on the matter of questions. Specifically, we can discover

(1) New (that is, *different*) answers to old questions.

(2) New questions.

(3) The inappropriateness or illegitimacy of our old questions.

With (1) we learn that the wrong answer has been given to an old question: we uncover an error of commission in our previous question-answering endeavors. With (2) we discover that there are certain questions that have not heretofore been posed at all: we uncover an error of omission in our former question-asking endeavors. Finally, with (3) we find that we have asked the wrong question altogether: we uncover an error of commission in our former question-asking endeavors, which are now seen to rest on incorrect presuppositions (and are thus generally bound up with type [1] discoveries). Three different sorts of cognitive progress are thus involved here – different from one another and from the traditional view of cognitive progress in terms of a straightforward "accretion of further knowledge."

The coming to be and passing away of questions is a phenomenon that can be mooted on this basis. A question *arises* at the time t if it then can meaningfully be posed because all its presuppositions are then taken to be true. And a question *dissolves* at t if one or another of its previously accepted presuppositions is no longer accepted. Any state of science will remove certain questions from the agenda and dismiss them as inappropriate. Newtonian dynamics dismissed the question "What cause is operative to keep a body in movement (with a uniform velocity in a straight line) once an impressed force has set it into motion?" Modern quantum theory does not allow us to ask "What caused this atom on californium to disintegrate after exactly 32.53 days, rather than, say, a day or two later?" Scientific questions should thus be regarded as arising in a *historical* setting. They arise at some juncture and not at others; they can be born and then die away.

A *change of mind* about the appropriate answer to some question will unravel the entire fabric of questions that presupposed this earlier answer. For if we change our mind regarding the correct answer to one member of a chain of questions, then the whole of a subsequent course of questioning may well collapse. If we abandon the luminiferous aether as a vehicle for electromagnetic radiation, then we lose at one stroke the whole host of questions about its composition, structure, mode of operation, origin, and so on. The course of erotetic change is no less dramatic than that of cognitive change.

Epistemic change over time thus relates not only to what is "*known*" but also to what can be *asked*. Newly secured information opens up new questions. And when the epistemic status of a presupposition changes from acceptance to abandonment or rejection, we witness the disappearance of various old presuppositions through dissolution. Questions regarding the *modus operandi* of phlogiston, the behavior of caloric fluid, the structure of the luminiferous aether, and the character of faster-than-light transmissions are all questions that have become lost to modern science because they involve presuppositions that have been abandoned.

The second of those aforementioned modes of erotetic discovery is particularly significant. The phenomenon of the "birth" of new questions was first emphasized by Immanuel Kant, who in his classic *Critique of Pure Reason* depicted the development of natural science in terms of a continually evolving cycle of questions and answers, where "*every answer given on principles of experience begets a fresh question, which likewise requires its answer* and thereby clearly shows the insufficiency of all scientific modes of explanation to satisfy reason."[1] This claim suggests the following Principle of Question Propagation – Kant's Principle, as we shall call it: "The answering of our factual (scientific) questions always paves the way to further as yet unanswered questions."

Note, however, that Kant's Principle can be construed in two rather different ways:

1. A *universalized* mode: EACH specific (particular) question Q that can be raised on a basis of a state-of-knowledge K engenders a (Q-correlative) line of questioning that leads ultimately to a question Q' whose answer lies outside of K – a question that forces an eventual shift from K to some suitably augmented or revised modification thereof.

2. A *particular* mode that arises when the capitalized EACH of the preceding formula is replaced by SOME.

On the first construction, science is an essentially divergent process, with questions leading to more questions in such a way that the erotetic agenda of successive stages of science continually grows in scope and size. This view was endorsed by W. Stanley Jevons, who wrote: "As it appears to me, the supply of new and unexplained facts is divergent in extent, so that the more we have explained, the more there is to explain."[2] The second construction is, however, a far more modest proposition, which merely sees science as self-perpetuating with some new questions arising at every stage, thereby opening a window of opportunity for the investigation of new issues. However, the question agenda of science is not necessarily a growing one, since questions may well die off by dissolution at a rate roughly equal to the birth of new questions.

[1] Immanuel Kant, *Prolegomena to Any Future Metaphysic*, sect. 57.
[2] W. S. Jevons, *Principles of Science,* 2nd ed. (London: Macmillan 1876), p. 753.

Kant himself undoubtedly intended the principle in the first (universalized) sense. But it would actually seem more plausible and realistic to adopt it in the second, more modest (particularized) sense, which yields a thesis amply supported by historical experience: that every state-of-the-art condition of questioning ultimately yields, somewhere along the road, a line of questioning that engenders the transition. The states of science are unstable: the natural course of inquiry provides an impetus by which a given state is ultimately led to give way to its successor. At bottom, Kant's Principle rests on the insight that no matter what answers are in hand, we can proceed to dig deeper into the how and why of things by raising yet further questions about the matters involved in these answers themselves. Accordingly, whenever we obtain new and different answers, interest is at once deflected to the issues they pose. When physicists postulate a new phenomenon they naturally want to know its character and modus operandi. When chemists synthesize a new substance they naturally want to know how it interacts with the old ones.

This Kantian principle of question-propagation in empirical inquiry indicates a fact of importance for the theory of cognitive progress. One need not claim longevity – let alone immortality – for any of the current problems to assure that there will be no problems ten or one hundred generations hence. (As immortal individuals are not needed to assure the immortality of the race, so immortal problems are not needed to assure the immortality of the scientific frontier.)

But what sort of reliance do we get on the development of new information with the cognitive progress of question resolution?

Edward Gibbon and Logarithmic Returns

As Spencer's Law of Cognitive Development would suggest, the *cognitive depth* of a body of information can be represented by its correlative taxonomy – by the elaborateness of the taxonomic structure that it engenders.[3] And on this basis, the preceding deliberations suggest that actual knowledge does not coordinate with the mere volume of

---

3 What concerns us here is emphatically not the "information" at issue in the theory of communication, which has nothing to do with the informative content of a message but only addresses its presentational complexity irrespective of the scope of its substantive content.

information but only with the systemic complexity it exhibits – and thereby with its logarithm. Accordingly, letting $K[I]$ represent the quantity of knowledge inherent in a body of information I of size #I, we have: $K[I] = \log \#I$.

And the purport of such a Law of Logarithmic Returns on expanding information is clear enough. To increase knowledge additively we must increase information multiplicatively: to advance knowledge by a single step we must enlarge the base of its information pyramid by a constant multiplicative factor.[4]

After all, not every insignificant smidgeon of information constitutes knowledge, and the person whose body of information consists of utter trivia really knows virtually nothing. To provide a simple illustration for this matter of significance, let us suppose an object-descriptive color taxonomy – for the sake of example, a very simple one based merely on Blue, Red, and Other. Then that single item of *knowledge* represented by "knowing the color" of an object – that it is red – is bound up with many different items of (correct) *information* on the subject (that it is not Blue, is rather similar to some shades of Other, etc.). As such information proliferates, we confront a situation of redundancy and diminished productiveness. Any knowable fact is always potentially surrounded by a vast prenumbral cloud of relevant information. And as our information becomes more extensive, those really *significant* facts become more difficult to discern.

Cognitive progress brings growing complexity in its wake. Its ongoing development involves us in ever-more free grained informative detail. Even as "little fleas have smaller fleas to bite 'em," so with issues settled at one level of generality there are deeply subordinated and thus smaller-scaled questions that are parasitically dependent on earlier ones. More information in greater detail is forthcoming, at an ever-accelerating pace, albeit at ever smaller orders of informative

---

[4] In information theory, *entropy* is the measure of the information conveyed by a message; it is measured by $k \log M$, where M is the number of structurally equivalent messages available via the available sorts of symbols. By extension, the present $\log I$ measure of the knowledge contained in a given body of information might accordingly be designated as the *enentropy*. Either way, the concept at issue measures informative actuality in relation to informative possibility. For there are two types of informative possibilities: (1) structural/syntactical as dealt with in classical information theory, and (2) hermeneutic/semantical (i.e., genuinely meaning-oriented) as dealt with in the present theory.

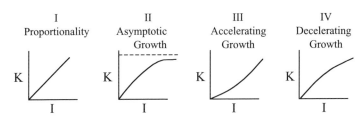

DISPLAY 4.1. The growth of knowledge in the wake of expanding information.

magnitude. But those increasingly fine-geared distinctions and sub-
tler considerations provide a diminishing informative yield. Thus a
vast amount of information can be exfoliated about any sort of thing
(be it a tree, a tool, or a person), but the really salient and significant knowledge of the item is generally something that can be set
out on a far more modest and small-scale basis. Our knowledge certainly increases with the addition of information but at a far less than
proportional rate.

A helpful perspective on this situation comes through the idea of
"noise": consider that expanding bodies of information encompass
so much unproductive redundancy and unhelpful irrelevancy that it
takes successive increases in information to effect successive fixed-size
increases in actual knowledge.

In theory, three sorts of relationships can be contemplated in the
development between information and knowledge – along the lines
depicted in Display 4.1. We have already seen that alternative I is untenable. So are II and III. The Law of Logarithmic Returns stipulates that
it is IV that actually obtains. It is not the most pessimistic alternative;
III clearly is. And it not the most optimistic; II clearly is – although IV,
like II, envisions a situation of ever-diminishing returns.

The Law of Logarithmic Returns is in line with – and is interest-
ingly illustrated by – the idea of a cognitive life span as expounded by
the sagacious Edward Gibbon (1737–94), the great historian of the
Roman republic. In his *Memoirs of My Life* he wrote: "The proportion
of a part to the whole is the only standard by which we can measure
the length of our existence. At the age of twenty, one year is a tenth
perhaps of the time which has elapsed within our consciousness and
memory; at the age of fifty it is no more than a fortieth, and this relative

value continues to decrease till the last sands are shaken out [of the hour-glass measure of our lifespan] by the hand of death."[5] On this basis, knowledge development is a matter of *adding a given percentage increment* to what has gone before. Thus fresh experience superadds its additional increment ΔE to the preexisting total E in such a way that its effective import is measured by the proportion that movement bears to the total: $\Delta E/E$. And cumulatively we of course have it that this comes to the logarithm of E: $\int \Delta E/E = \log E$. On such an approach, an increment to one's lifetime has a *cognitive* value determined on strict analogy with Daniel Bernoulli's famous proposal to measure the *utility* value of incremental economic resources by means of a logarithmic yardstick.

Derek Price designated a "scholar's solidness" – his stature as a contributor to his field – as the logarithm of his life's total of publications.[6] But, as he himself suggests in passing, we might just as well expand this from the individual to the community, and use it to measure not just the productivity of a person but also the aggregate of total contributions in a field. And in taking this step, we once again reach a logarithmic measure of "cognitive solidarity" that would – as already noted – qualify as a measure of the overall knowledge that the field encompasses.

To be sure, a devotee of Thomas Kuhn's *The Structure of Scientific Revolutions*[7] might suggest that logarithmic retardation occurs only within the routine ("normal") phases of scientific development whereas the revolutions that periodically lift science to a new level see a sprint forward with new findings rushing in. But this view is overoptimistic in ignoring the increasingly vast labor need to lift the science from one level to the next. For a realistic picture see Display 4.2, which conveys some idea of how such a process would proceed. And it shows graphically that a Kuhnian view of spirit-penetrated scientific progress is nowise at odds with the logarithmic retardation inherent in Gibbon's Law. The Kuhnian picture of new paradigms of scientific

---

[5] Edward Gibbon, *Memoirs of My Life* (Harmondworth, 1984), p. 63. Gibbon's "law of learning" thus means that a body of experience that grows linearly over time yields a merely logarithmic growth in *cognitive* age. Thus a youngster of 10 years has attained only one-eighth of his or her expected *chronological* life span but has already passed the halfway mark of his or her expected *cognitive* life span.

[6] Derek J. Price, *Little Science, Big Science* (New York: Columbia University Press, 1963), p. 50.

[7] Thomas Kuhn, *The Structure of Scientific Revolutions* (Chicago: University of Chicago Press, 1962).

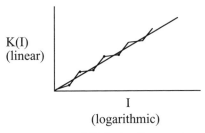

DISPLAY 4.2. A Kuhnian Perspective.

understanding opening up the prospect of periodic leaps in progress followed by a logarithmic phase of "moral science" is perfectly compatible with the present account.[8]

Gibbon's Law means that an immense mass of information stands coordinate with a modest body of knowledge. From the standpoint of knowledge, information is highly redundant. Consider an example. The yield of knowledge from information afforded by legibility impaired manuscripts and papyri and inscriptions in classical paleography provides an instructive instance. If we can decipher 70 percent of its letters we can generally identify the text at issue in such a manuscript. If we can make out 70 percent of its phases we can pretty well figure out a sentence. If we can read 70 percent of its sentences we can understand the message of the whole text. Some one-third of the letters suffice to carry the whole message. So the mass of information at hand boils down to a far smaller amount of knowledge. And this sort of situation has far-reaching implications for the progress of knowledge.

One instructive way to measure the volume of available information is through the opportunities for placement in a framework for describing or classifying the features of things. With n concepts, you can make n^2 two-concept combinations. With m facts, you can project m^2 fact-connecting juxtapositions, in each of which some sort of characteristic relationship is at issue. A single step in the advancement of knowledge is here accompanied by a massive increase in the proliferation of information. Extending the previous example, let us also contemplate *shapes* in addition to *colors*, again supposing only three of

---

[8] For a fuller treatment of the relevant issues see the author's *Scientific Progress* (Oxford: Blackwell, 1978), especially chapters X–XIII.

them: rectangular, circular, other. Now when we *combine* color and shape there will be $9 = 3 \times 3$ possibilities in the resultant (cross-) classification. So with that complex, dual-aspect piece of knowledge (color + shape) we also launch into a vastly amplified (i.e., multiplied) information spectrum over that increased classification-space. In moving cognitively from n to $n + 1$ cognitive parameters we enlarge our knowledge additively but expand our information field multiplicatively.

If a control mechanism can handle three items – be it in physical or in cognitive management – then we can lift ourselves to higher levels of capacity by hierarchical layering. First we can, by hypothesis, manage three base-level items; next we can, by grouping three of these into a first-level complex, manage nine base-level items; and thereupon by grouping three of these first-level complexes into a second-level complex we can manage 27 base-level items. Hierarchical grouping is thus clearly a pathway to enhanced managerial capacity. But in cognitive contexts of information management it is clear that a few items of high-level information (= knowledge) can and will correspond to a vast range of low-level information (= mere truths). Knowing (in our illustration) where we stand within each of those three levels – that is, having three pieces of *knowledge* – will position us in a vastly greater information space (one of 27 compartments). And this situation is typical. The relational structure of the domain means that a small range of knowledge (by way of specifically high-grade information) can always serve to position one cognitively within a vastly greater range of low-level information.

It is also instructive to view this idea from a different point of view. Knowledge commonly develops via distinctions (A vs. non-A) that are introduced with ever-greater elaboration to address the problems and difficulties that one encounters with less sophisticated approaches. A situation obtains that is analogous to the "Game of 20 Questions" with an exponentially exfoliating possibility space being traced out stepwise $(2, 4, 8, 16, \ldots, 2^n, \ldots)$. With n descriptors one can specify for 2^n potential descriptions that specify exactly how, over all, a given object may be characterized. When we add a new descriptor we increase by one additional unit the amount of knowledge but double the amount of available information. The *information* at hand grows with 2^n, but the knowledge acquired merely with n. The cognitive exploitation of information is a matter of dramatically diminishing returns.

#I	cI (with c = .1)	log cI (=K[I])	Δ (K[I])	K[I] as % of #I
100	10	1	–	1.0
1,000	100	2	1	.2
10,000	1000	3	1	.03
100,000	10,000	4	1	.004

DISPLAY 4.3. The structure of the knowledge/information relation.

And so, as Display 4.3 illustrates, there is a substantial imbalance between the magnitation of $K[I]$ and #I itself, and with ever-increasing information, the corresponding increase in knowledge shrinks markedly.[9] To increase knowledge by equal steps we must amplify information by successive orders of magnitude. Each time we double our mere information we increase our knowledge by only one single step. The cognitive exploitation of information is a matter of dramatically diminishing returns. The difference at issue is that between merely linear and drastically exponential growth. For linear growth increases what has gone before by a fixed *amount* per period; exponential growth increases what has gone before by a fixed *percentage* per period. And the difference is of course drastic.

The Law of Logarithmic Returns thus presents us with an epistemological analogue of the old Weber-Fechner law of psychophysics, asserting that inputs of geometrically increasing magnitude are required to yield *perceptual* outputs of arithmetically increasing intensity, for the presently contemplated law envisions a parallelism of perception and conception in this regard. It stipulates that (informational) inputs of geometrically increasing magnitude are needed to provide for (cognitive and thus) *conceptual* outputs of arithmetically increasing magnitude. And so Gibbon's Law of Logarithmic Returns as a principle of the realm of *conception* parallels the Weber-Fechner Law in the epistemics of *perception*. In searching for meaningful patterns, the ongoing proliferation of data-points makes contributions of rapidly diminishing value.[10]

It is not too difficult to come by a plausible explanation for the sort of information/knowledge relationship that is represented by

[9] Throughout this book the symbol # will represent a numerical content measure contrast functions in such a way that, given any set S, #S will represent the conditionality of the membership of S.

[10] On the relevance of the Weber-Fechner law to scientometrics see Derek Price, *Little Science, Big Science*, pp. 50–51.

$K[I] = \log \#I$. One good reason for such a $K[I]/\#I$ imbalance may lie in the efficiency of intelligence in securing a view of the *modus operandi* of a world whose law-structure is sufficiently simple to be learner friendly – at least in part. For then one can extract a disproportionate amount of general fact from a modest amount of information. (Note that whenever an infinite series of 0's and 1's, as per 01010101 ..., is generated – as this sample series indeed is – by a relatively *simple* law, then this circumstance can be gleaned from a comparatively short initial segment of this series.) In rational inquiry we try the simple solutions first, and when they cease to work – when they are ruled out by further findings (by some further influx of coordinating information) – we move on to the more complex. Things go along smoothly until an over-simple solution becomes destabilized by enlarged experience. We get by with the comparatively simpler options until we have to do otherwise by the expanding information about the world's *modus operandi* made possible through enhanced new means of observation and experimentation. But with the expansion of knowledge, new accessions mean new demands. At bottom, then, there are two closely interrelated reasons for that disparity between $K[I]$ and #I. For one thing, where order exists in the world, intelligence is rather efficient in finding it. And for another, if the world were not orderly – were not amenable to the probes of intelligence – then intelligent beings would not and could not have emerged in it through evolutionary mechanisms.

The circumstance that ample information yields only modest knowledge must not be invoked as an argument for skepticism as this doctrine is usually understood. For, of course, skepticism as usually conceived maintains that the realization of knowledge is *infeasible*, whereas the line of thought that is presently at issue hold that it is *difficult and challenging*. What is at issue here is that the obstacles to knowledge are substantial, not that they are insurmountable.

Diminishing Returns and Logarithmic Retardation

Consider now the result of combining two ideas:

(1) Knowledge is distinguished from mere information as such by its significance. In fact, *knowledge is simply particularly significant information* – information whose significance exceeds some threshold level (say q). (In principle

there is room for variation here according as one sets the quality level of entry qualification and the domain higher or lower.)

(2) The significance of *additional* information is determined by its impact on *preexisting* information. Significance in this sense is a matter of the relative (percentage-wise) increase that the new acquisitions effect upon the body of preexisting information (I), which may – to reiterate – be estimated in the first instance by the sheer volume of the relevant body of information: the literature of the subject.

Accordingly, *the significance of incrementally new information can be measured in terms of how much it adds, and thus by the* ratio *of the increment of new information to the volume of information already in hand:* Δ #I/#I. Thus knowledge constituting *significant* information is determined through the proportional extent of the change effected by a new item in the preexisting situation (independently of what that preexisting situation is). In milking additional information for cognitively significant insights it is generally the *proportion* of the increase that matters: its percentage rather than its brute amount. So here too we arrive at the Law of Logarithmic Returns governing the extraction of significant *knowledge* from bodies of mere *information*.

On this basis of this fundamental relationship, the knowledge of a two-sector domain increases additively notwithstanding a multiplicative explosion in the amount of information that is now on the scene. For if the field (*F*) under consideration consists of two sub-fields (*F*1 and *F*2), then because of the cross-connections obtaining within the information-domains at issue the overall information complex will take on a multiplicative size:

$$\text{\#I} = inf(F) = inf(F_1) \times inf(F_2) = \text{\#I}_1 \times \text{\#I}_2.$$

With compilation, information is multiplied. But in view of the indicated logarithmic relationship, the knowledge associated with the body of compound information *I* will stand at

$$K[I] = \log \text{\#I} = \log(\text{\#I}_1 \times \text{\#I}_2) = \log \text{\#I}_1 + \log \text{\#I}_2 = K[I_1] + K[I_2].$$

The knowledge obtained by compiling two information-domains (subfields) into an overall aggregate will (as one would expect) consist simply in *adding* the two bodies of knowledge at issue. Where compilation increases *information* by multiplicative leaps and bounds, the increase in *knowledge* is merely additive.

It is not too difficult to come by a plausible explanation for the sort of information/knowledge relationship that is represented by $K = \log I$. The principal reason for such a K/I imbalance may lie in the efficiency of intelligence in securing a view of the *modus operandi* of a world whose law-structure is comparatively simple. For here one can learn a disproportionate amount of general fact from a modest amount of information. (Note that whenever an infinite series of 0's and 1's, as per 01010101 . . . , is generated – as this series indeed is – by a relatively *simple* law, then this circumstance can be gleaned from a comparatively short initial segment of the series.) In rational inquiry we try the simple solutions first, and only when they cease to work – when they are ruled out by further findings (by some further influx of coordinating information) – do we move on to the more complex. Things go along smoothly until an over simple solution becomes destabilized by the enlarged experience afforded us by enhanced new means of observation and experimentation.

The implications for cognitive progress of this disparity between knowledge and mere information are not difficult to discern. Nature imposes increasing resistance barriers to intellectual as to physical penetration. Consider the analogy of extracting air for creating a vacuum. The first 90 percent comes out rather easily. The next 9 percent is as difficult to extract as all that went before. The next .9 is proportionally just as difficult. And so on. Each successive order-of-magnitude step involves a massive cost for lesser progress; each successive fixed-size investment of effort yields a substantially diminished return.

The circumstance that the increase of information carries with it a merely logarithmic return in point of increased knowledge suggests that nature imposes a resistance barrier to intellectual as well as to physical penetration. Intellectual progress is exactly the same: when we extract actual *knowledge* (i.e., high-grade, descriptively significant information) from mere information of the routine, common "garden variety," the same sort of quantity/quality relationship obtains. Initially a sizable proportion of the available is high grade – but as we press further this proportion of what is cognitively significant gets ever smaller. To double knowledge we must quadruple information. As science progresses, the important discoveries that represent real increases in knowledge are surrounded by a growing penumbra of mere items of information. (The mathematical literature of the day yields an annual crop of over 200,000 new theorems.)[11]

Planck's Principle

In the ongoing course of scientific progress, the earlier investigations in the various departments of inquiry are able to skim the cream, so to speak: they take the "easy pickings," and later achievements of comparable significance require deeper forays into complexity and call for much larger bodies of information. (It is important to realize that this cost-increase is not because latter-day workers are doing *better* science, but simply because it is harder to achieve *the same level* of science: one must dig deeper or search wider to achieve results of the same significance as before.) This situation is reflected in Max Planck's appraisal of the problems of scientific progress. He wrote that "*with every advance [in science] the difficulty of the task is increased; ever larger demands are made on the achievements of researchers,* and the need for a suitable division of labor becomes more pressing."[12] The Law of Logarithmic Returns would at once characterize and explain this circumstance of what can be termed Planck's Principle of Increasing Effort to the effect that substantial findings are easier to come by in the earlier phase of a new discipline and become more difficult in the natural course of progress.

A great deal of impressionistic and anecdotal evidence certainly points toward the increasing costs of high-level science. Scientists frequently complain that "all the easy research has been done."[13] The need for increasing specialization and division of labor is but one indication of this. A devotee of scientific biography cannot help noting the disparity between the immense output and diversified fertility in

---

[11] See Stanislaw M. Ulam, *Adventures of a Mathematician* (New York: Scribner's, 1976).

[12] Max Planck, *Vorträge und Erinnerungen*, 5th ed. (Stuttgart, 1949), p. 376, italics added. Shrewd insights seldom go unanticipated, so it is not surprising that other theorists should be able to contest claims to Planck's priority here. C. S. Peirce is particularly noteworthy in this connection.

[13] See William George, *The Scientist in Action* (New York: Arno Press, 1938), p. 307. The sentiment is not new. George Gore vainly lambasted it 100 years ago: "Nothing can be more puerile than the complaints sometimes made by certain cultivators of a science, that it is very difficult to make discoveries now that the soil has been exhausted, whereas they were so easily made when the ground was first broken." George Gore, *The Art of Scientific Discovery* (London: Macmillan, 1878), p. 21.

the productive careers of the scientific collosi of earlier days and the more modest scope of the achievements of their successors. As science progresses within any of its established branches, there is a marked increase in the overall resource-cost of realizing scientific findings of a given level of intrinsic significance (by essentially absolutistic standards of importance).[14] At first one can skim the cream, so to speak: take the "easy pickings." But later achievements of comparable significance require deeper forays into complexity and an ever-greater investment of effort and material resources.[15]

The idea that science is not only subject to a principle of escalating costs but also to a law of diminishing returns is due to the nineteenth-century American philosopher of science Charles Sanders Peirce (1839–1914). In his pioneering 1878 essay on "Economy of Research" Peirce put the issue in the following terms:

> We thus see that when an investigation is commenced, after the initial expenses are once paid, at little cost we improve our knowledge, and improvement then is especially valuable; but as the investigation goes on, additions to our knowledge cost more and more, and, at the same time, are of less and less worth. All the sciences exhibit the same phenomenon, and so does the course of life. At first we learn very easily, and the interest of experience is very great; but it becomes harder and harder, and less and less worthwhile.
>
> (*Collected Papers*, Vol. VII [Cambridge, MA, 1958], sect. 7.144)

More information will always yield more knowledge – but simply less of it. The increase of knowledge over time stands to the increase

---

[14] The following passage offers a clear token of the operation of this principle specifically with respect to chemistry: Over the past ten years the expenditures for basic chemical research in universities have increased at a rate of about 15 per cent per annum; much of the increase has gone for superior instrumentation, [and] for the staff needed to service such instruments. . . . Because of the expansion in research opportunities, the increased cost of the instrumentation required to capitalize on these opportunities, and the more highly skilled supporting personnel needed for the solution of more difficult problems, the cost of each individual research problem in chemistry is rising rapidly. (F. H. Wertheimer et al., *Chemistry: Opportunities and Needs* [Washington, DC, 1965; National Academy of Sciences/National Research Council], p. 17.)

[15] The talented amateur has virtually been driven out of science. In 1881 the Royal Society included many fellows in this category (with Darwin, Joule, and Spottiswoode among the more distinguished of them). Today there are no amateurs. See D. S. C. Cardwell, "The Professional Society" in Norman Kaplan (ed.), *Science and Society* (Chicago: University of Chicago Press, 1965), pp. 86–91 (see p. 87).

of information in a proportion fixed by the *inverse* of the volume of already available information:

$$\frac{d}{dt}K[I] \approx \frac{d}{dt}\log \#I \approx \frac{1}{\#I}\frac{d}{dt}\#I.$$

The more knowledge we already have in hand, the slower (by very rapid decline) will be the rate at which knowledge grows with newly acquired information. And the larger the body of available information, the smaller will be the proportion of this information that represents real knowledge.

The Law of Logarithmic Returns thus has substantial implications for the *rate* of scientific progress.[16] We cannot hope to predict the *content* of future science, but the knowledge/information relationship does put us in a position to make plausible estimates about its *volume*. There is no inherent limit to the possibility of future progress in scientific knowledge, but the exploitation of this theoretical prospect becomes more difficult, expensive, and demanding in terms of effort and ingenuity. New findings of equal significance require greater aggregate efforts. Accordingly, the historical situation has been one of a *constant* progress of science as a *cognitive discipline* notwithstanding its *exponential* growth as a *productive enterprise* (as measured in terms of resources, money, manpower, publications, etc.).[17] If we look at the cognitive situation of science in its quantitative aspect, the Law of Logarithmic Returns pretty much says it all. In this perspective, the struggle to achieve cognitive mastery over nature presents a succession of escalating demands, with the exponential growth in the *enterprise* associated with a merely linear growth in the *discipline*. But do the facts bear this out?

---

[16] One might ask: "Why should a mere accretion in scientific 'information' – in mere belief – be taken to constitute *progress*, seeing that those later beliefs are not necessarily *true* (even as the earlier ones were not)?" The answer is that they are in any case better *substantiated* – that they are "improvements" on the earlier ones by the elimination of shortcomings. For a more detailed consideration of the relevant issues, see the author's *Scientific Realism* (Dordrecht: D. Reidel, 1987).

[17] We are caught up here in the usual cyclic pattern of all hypothetico-deductive reasoning, in addition to explaining the various phenomena we have been canvassing that projected K/I relationship is in turn substantiated by them. This is not a vicious circularity but simply a matter of the systemic coherence that lies at the basis of inductive reasonings. Of course the crux is that there should also be some predictive power, which is exactly what our discussion of deceleration is designed to exhibit.

5

Adams's Thesis on Exponential Growth

(1) There should, of course, be sure empirical confirmation for Gibbon's Law. (2) And this can be found in the observation of Henry Adams that recent history has seen an exponential growth in scientific activity – and correlatively in information as well. (3) This phenomenon is substantiated on many sides. (4) However, there is also good reason to think that the expansion of scientific knowledge has proceeded throughout this period at a merely linear (rather than exponential) rate. (5) It emerges on this basis that knowledge stands not as the volume of information but merely as its logarithm. So viewed in this light, the development of modern science amply substantiates Gibbon's Law of Logarithmic Returns. (Appendix) A conspectus of relevant literature.

Scientific Progress

It is instructive also to consider the information/knowledge relationship from the angle of history. In developmental perspective, there is good reason to suppose that our body of bare *information* will increase more or less in proportion with our resource investment in information gathering. Accordingly, since this investment grows exponentially over time (as has historically been the case in the recent period), we have it that

$$\#I(t) \propto c^t \text{ and correspondingly also } \frac{d}{dt}\#I(t) \approx c^t.$$

(Note that here $x \approx y$ means that $x = cy$ for some constant c, and $x \propto cy + y$ for constants c and k.) Given Gibbon's Law of Logarithmic

Returns, this just-indicated relationship means

$$K[I(t)] = \log \#I(t) \approx \log c^t \approx t$$

and consequently

$$\frac{d}{dt}K[I(t)] = \text{constant}.$$

It follows on this basis that, since *exponential* growth in *I* is coordinated with a merely *linear* growth in $K[I]$, the rate of scientific progress in point of knowledge during the information-exploding past has actually remained essentially constant.

But do the observed facts bear this out? The preceding discussion has argued for Gibbon's Law $K[I] = \log \#I$ on the basis of general principles. But will the historical data provide empirical substantiation for it? Let us examine the issue.

Adams's Thesis

Knowledge is an unusual resource; it is one of those very rare commodities that are not diminished but rather amplified through consumption. This makes the growth of knowledge a potentially explosive process, and by the end of the nineteenth century no clear-eyed observer could fail to remark the striking pace of scientific advance. Among the first to detail this phenomenon in exact terms by endeavoring to give it mathematical formulation was Henry Brooks Adams (1838–1918), the American scholar, historian, and student of cultural affairs. (He was a grandson of John Adams, George Washington's successor as president.) Noting that scientific work increased at a rate fixed by a constant doubling time – so that science has an *exponential* growth-rate – Adams characterized this circumstance as a "law of acceleration" governing the progress of science. He wrote:

Laplace would have found it child's play to fix a ratio in the progression in mathematical science between Descartes, Leibnitz, Newton and himself.... Pending agreement between.... authorities, theory may assume what it likes – say a fifty or even a five-and-twenty year period of reduplication. . . . for the period matters little once the acceleration itself is admitted.[1]

Roughly speaking, Adams envisaged science as doubling in size and content with every succeeding half-century, producing a situation of exponential growth. And Adams did not stand alone here, as an anticipation of his idea occurred in an *obiter dictum* in the 1901 Presidential Address to the British Association for the Advancement of Science by William Thomson (Lord Kelvin):

Scientific wealth tends to accumulate according to the law of compound interest. Every addition to knowledge of the properties of matter supplies the naturalist with new instrumental means for discovering and interpreting phenomena of nature, which in their turn afford foundations for fresh generalizations.[2]

Anticipations notwithstanding, the thesis that science develops under compound-interest conditions with the effect of a continually accelerating – indeed an exponential – growth rate may properly be designated as *Adams's Thesis of Exponential Growth*. It amounts to the claim that the *percentage rate of the per annum increase in the levels of scientific effort and quantitative productivity remains constant with the passage of time.*[3] Adams characterized his principle as a "law of acceleration, definite and constant as any law of mechanics [which] cannot be supposed to relax its energy to suit the convenience of man."[4]

---

[1] *The Education of Henry Adams* (Boston, 1918; privately printed in 1907), chapter 34 (see p. 491). This chapter was written in 1904.

[2] See Kelvin's address in G. Basalla, William Coleman, and R. H. Kargon (eds.), *Victorian Science: A Self-Portrait through the Presidential Addresses of the British Association for the Advancement of Science* (New York: New York Academy of Science, 1970), pp. 101–28 (see p. 114, and compare p. 488). The idea also occurs in embryonic form in A. Conan Doyle's 1894 short story *The Great Keinplatz Experiment*, which claims that "knowledge begets knowledge as money bears interest."

[3] The exponential growth of a quantity – its growth at "compound interest" – is governed by the principle that at any time the rate of growth is proportional to the (then extant) volume. It produces fixed doubling times (or tripling times, etc.), and sequential fixed-period augmentations that increase in a geometric ratio.

[4] *The Education of Henry Adams*, p. 493. For an interesting discussion of Adams's numerous, complex, and changing ideas regarding scientific and intellectual progress see Ernest Samuels, *Henry Adams: The Major Phase* (Cambridge, MA: Harvard University Press, 1964).

The historical facts bear Adams out in this regard. For irrespective of whether S represents scientific literature or manpower or information, the growth of the enterprise has been exponential. Throughout recent history it transpires that[5]

$$S \propto e^t \text{ or equivalently} \log S \propto t.$$

And this, in effect, is the purport of Adams's Thesis.

Dimensions of the Phenomenon

When Henry Adams enunciated his "law of acceleration," he did so on the basis of shrewd perception and hunch based on informal insight into the historical course of things. Only a few scattered fragments of statistical information needed to substantiate the historical reality of this phenomenon were available in his day. However, this situation is nowadays greatly improved. The continued data-gathering effort of statisticians, sociologists, historians of science, and science administrators provide impressive documentation of the phenomenon discerned by Adams.[6] Let us examine some of its dimensions.

Manpower

In 1875 the American Association for the Advancement of Science had 807 members. Since then its membership has increased by leaps and bounds into the tens of thousands. The register of *American Men of Science* commenced publication in 1903 and exhibits a comparable history of exponential growth. During most of the present century the number of doctrinal scientists in the United States has been increasing at around 6 percent yearly to yield an exponential growth rate with a doubling time of roughly 12 years.[7] (In the U.K. the comparable figures stand at some 4 percent and 18 years, respectively.)[8] A startling consideration that is often but deservedly repeated is that well over 80 percent of ever-existing scientists (in even the oldest specialties,

---

[5] We here use the notation $x \approx y$ for $x = cy$ and $x \propto y$ for $x = cy + k$. The former represents a relation of strictly linear proportionality; the latter represents the same apart from the positioning of the origin.

[6] For details regarding the literature see the Bibliographic Appendix to this chapter.

[7] See, e.g., Derek J. Price, *Little Science, Big Science*, p. 11. This holds in virtually every field of exact natural science.

[8] *Statistics of Science and Technology* (London: HMSO, 1970), p. 115.

e.g., mathematics, physics, and medicine) are alive and active at the present time.

Literature and Information

First, a bit of hermeneutics. Scientific knowledge is coordinated, interconnected, and systematized. It is predicated on providing information about how things are interrelated and interconnected. Now consider any system of n elements. There will, in principle, obtain between these items $n \times (n - 1)$ interconnections. But let a new element be brought on the scene. In its wake there will now be $(n + 1) \times n$ interconnections in the new state of things that has come to obtain. Accordingly, the shift from n to $n + 1$ that has been engendered by the progress represented by the introduction of that one single new item has increased our cognitive system by $2n$. A single step forward has thus seen an increase in the field of information by an amount proportionate to the size of the body of knowledge that was already at hand. In other words, we have exponential growth.

Deliberations along these lines indicate that as further elements are introduced into the range of our cognitive horizons the amount of raw information with which we have to cope will grow exponentially. Little wonder, then, that exactly this sort of thing is what has been happening in the realm of reference works, of scientific and scholarly journals, of libraries, and of the information domain of electronic search engines.

In regard to the literature of science, it is readily documented that – as Display 5.1 indicated – the number of books, of journals, and of journal papers has been increasing exponentially over the recent period,[9] with scientific information growing at an average of some 5 percent annually throughout the last two centuries. The result is exponential growth with a doubling time of ca. 15 years – an order-of-magnitude increase roughly every half century. By 1960, some 300,000 different book titles were being published in the world, and the two decades from 1955 and 1975 saw the doubling of titles published in Europe

---

[9] Cf. Derek J. Price, *Science since Babylon*, 2nd ed. (New Haven, CT: Yale University Press, 1975), and also *Characteristics of Doctrinal Scientists and Engineers in the University System*, 1991 (Arlington, VA: National Science Foundation, 1994), Document No. 94–307.

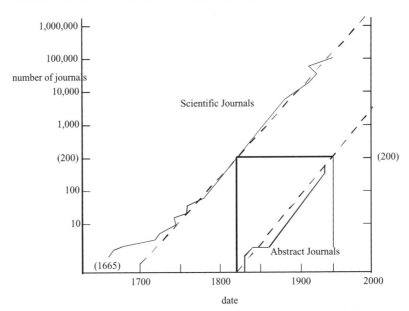

DISPLAY 5.1. The number of scientific journals and abstract journals founded, as a function of date. *Source*: Derek J. Solla Price, *Science since Babylon* (New Haven: Yale University Press, 1961).

from around 130,000 to over 270,000,[10] and science has had its full share of this literature explosion. The result is a veritable flood of scientific literature. It is reliably estimated that, from the start, about 10 million scientific papers have been published, and currently some 30,000 journals publish some 600,000 new papers each year.

Facilities and Expenditure

Research and development expenditures in the United States grew exponentially after World War II, increasing at a rate of some 10 percent per annum. By the mid-1960s, America was spending more on scientific research and development than the entire federal budget before Pearl Harbor.

And America has not been alone here. Throughout the world, the proliferation of scientific facilities has proceeded at an impressive pace over the past hundred years. (In the early 1870s there were only 11

---

[10] Data from *An International Survey of Book Production during the Last Decades* (Paris: UNESCO, 1985).

physics laboratories in the British Isles; by the mid 1930s there were more than 300; today there are several thousand.)[11] And, of course, the scale of activities in these laboratories has also expanded vastly. The immense cost in resources of the research equipment of contemporary science is well known; even large organizations can hardly continue to keep pace with the rising levels of research expenditures.[12] Radiotelescopic observatories, low-temperature physics, research hospitals, and lunar geology all involve outlays on a scale that requires the funding support of national governments – sometimes even consortia thereof. Science has become a vastly expensive undertaking. In a prophetic voice, Alvin M. Weinberg (then Director of the Oak Ridge National Laboratory) wrote:

When history looks at the 20th century, she will see science and technology as its theme; she will find in the monuments of Big Science – the huge rockets, the high-energy accelerators, the high flux research reactors – symbols of our time just as surely as she finds in Notre Dame a symbol of the Middle Ages.[13]

The expansion of scientific activity – and cost! – throughout the 20th century has been one of the characteristic phenomena of the era.

The Linear Growth of Knowledge

But let us now turn attention from scientific *effort* to scientific *progress*. The picture that confronts us here is not quite so expansive. There is good reason that *the substantive level of scientific innovation has remained roughly constant over the last few generations*. This contention – that while

---

[11] Data from William George, *The Scientist in Action* (London: Williams & Norgate, 1938).

[12] Du Pont's outlays for research stood at $1 million *per annum* during World War I (1915–1918), $6 million in 1930, $38 million in 1950, and $96 million in 1960. (Data from Fritz Machlup, *The Production and Distribution of Knowledge in the United States* [Princeton: Princeton University Press, 1962], pp. 158–59; and see pp. 159–60 for the relevant data on a larger scale.) Overall expenditures for scientific research and its technological development (R&D) in the United States stood at $.11 × 10^9 in 1920, $.13 × 10^9 in 1930, $.38 × 10^9 in 1940, $2.9 × 10^9 in 1950, $5.1 × 10^9 in 1953–54, $10.0 × 10^9 in 1957–58, $11.1 × 10^9 in 1958–59, and ca. $14.0 × 10^9 in 1960–61 (ibid., pp. 155 and 187). Machlup thinks it a not unreasonable conjecture that no other industry or economic activity in the United States has grown as fast as R&D (ibid., p. 155).

[13] "The Impact of Large-Scale Science on the United States," *Science*, 134 (1961; 21 July issue), 161–64 (see p. 161).

scientific *efforts* have grown exponentially the production of really high-level scientific *findings* has remained constant – admits of various substantiating considerations.

The number of scientists and the number of scientific publications has increased roughly 10-fold every 50 years since the 17th century; on that basis, one would say that the sum total of scientific knowledge has seen a one-unit increase during every half century of recent history.[14] One indicator of this constancy in high-quality science is the relative stability of honors (medals, prizes, honorary degrees, membership of scientific academics, etc.). In some instances these reflect a fixed-number situation (e.g., Nobel prizes in natural science). But if the volume of clearly first-rate scientific work were expanding drastically, there would be mounting pressure for the enlargement of such honorific awards and mounting discontent with the inequity of the present reward-system. There are no signs of this.

Another significant indication of a merely linear increase in scientific progress relates to references to specific findings – references not in "the literature" at large, but in the synoptic handbooks, monographs, and treatises that endeavor to give a rounded picture of "the state of the discipline." The indices to such works have increased only linearly.

Yet another sign of a merely linear growth of knowledge in spite of an exponential increase in information emerges from the study of citations. The scientific literature has been growing at an exponential rate in the modern era, subject to a doubling time of roughly 15 years; nevertheless, the proportion of contributions that are of sufficient importance to be cited in the later literature declined greatly.[15] Specifically, publications among a given annual crop that are cited at least once within a fixed interval (the *persisting* citations, so to speak) has also been shrinking by one-half every 15 years. Correspondingly – albeit not coincidentally – the number of persistents among the given year's

---

[14] Compare Price, *Little Science, Big Science*, pp. 55–56.

[15] Citations are doubtless problematic as a measure of merit. All the same, citation indices can surely be exploited to yield a fairly good indication of statistical trends. Thus a reasonable indication of a paper's utility would be its citation in a reasonable proportion of papers in its field within a suitable time after its publication. Of course, this utility might be practical/experimental rather than cognitive/theoretical. But ways can always be devised to make allowances for such cases.

crop is constant. In other words, while the literature grows exponentially, the added number of significant results (as estimated by those citation persistents) remains constant over time.[16] And the citation evidence also indicates that science *as a body of knowledge* has grown at a merely linear rate.[17]

In the end, it should not be all that surprising that the pace of authentically cognitive progress should remain constant even during a time of dramatic information growth. After all, if an important, really outstanding result in some field of inquiry is one (as is usually the case) that *is cited in X percent of the literature,* then the number of important contributions can (and generally will) remain constant over an exponential growth of the literature simply because the bar of qualification is here being raised in proportion with the literature itself.

Specifically, consider the following:

The citation-prominent members of a literature L – let this be *prom*(L) – are those cited by at least some fixed fraction thereof (say 1%).

Now in this regard, citation studies of the scientific literature show that a linear relationship obtains between #L and #*prom*(L) on log-log graphing:[18]

$$\log \#L \approx \log \# \, prom(L)$$

This means that

$$\log(k \times \#L) = \log \, prom(k \times \#L).$$

But we then have

$$\log(k \times \#L) = \log k + \log \#L \propto \log \#L \approx \log \# \, prom(L).$$

In other words, as L increases multiplicatively, prom (L) increases additively.

A host of relevant considerations thus conspire to indicate that when science grows exponentially as a productive *enterprise,* its growth as an intellectual *discipline* proceeds at a merely *constant* and *linear* pace.

---

[16] For the data that substantiate this line of reasoning, see Price, *Little Science, Big Science,* pp. 79–80.

[17] Recall that in speaking of accumulation here, we have in mind enlargement in the number of "significant results" whose contents may be in no sense cumulative.

[18] For further detail see Price, *Little Science, Big Science.*

The Lesson

At this point a significant conclusion comes into view. Let us put the pieces together. The situation represented by Adams's Thesis indicates an *exponential* growth of scientific *information* in recent times. On the other hand, a closer look at scientific *understanding* in terms of the *knowledge* that represents our depth of understanding indicates a merely constant growth throughout this recent period. And this combination tells the story. If an *exponential* growth in information stands propositional to a merely *linear* growth of the correlative knowledge, then it indeed follows that $\#K = \log \#I$, just as specified by Gibbon's Law. This of course means that as an information domain expands exponentially – as is the case during an Adams's Law era exponential scientific expansion – those top-quality findings that represent the growth of knowledge will increase merely linearly. Thus there is, as we have seen, good reason to think that this is actually the case, and the available data do indeed substantiate the Gibbon's Law relationship between information and knowledge.[19]

Bibliographic Appendix

The first to take up Adams's Thesis in a serious way on the basis of statistical data was F. K. Richtmyer, who, on analyzing the review literature in physics, concluded that "since its beginning physics has increased, with each generation, in a geometrical ratio."[20] In due course, the idea became commonplace:

> The time scale of human progress is certainly not linear. Technical progress grows more rapid as time goes on, and perhaps the best chronological scale for the history of science and technology would be one in which the divisions of the scale were proportional to the logarithms of their distance from the present time.[21]

---

[19] What of the future? If it requires an exponential increase in scientific work and information to achieve a merely linear growth in scientific knowledge, what can be expected in a future in which there is at best a steady-state constancy in resource investment in science? Here Gibbon's law $K = \log I$ implies what might be called a *logarithmic retardation* in the price of scientific growth with ever-larger entailment between the achievement of significant breakthroughs. The case for this view of things has been argued in the author's *Scientific Progress* (Oxford: Blackwell, 1978).

[20] "The Romance of the Next Decimal Place," *Science,* 75 (1932), p. 1–5 (see pp. 1–2).

[21] C. E. K. Mees, *The Path of Science* (New York: Wiley & Sons, 1946), p. 21.

However, the documentation of Adams's Law improved greatly in the early 1950s. On the side of *outputs* (i.e., scientific papers) a pioneer study was Derek J. Price's "Quantitative Measures of the Development of Science," *Archives internationales d'Histoire des Sciences,* vol. 14 (1951), pp. 85–93, which maintained that the literature of science has grown with a doubling time of some 12 years (a period that seems a bit too small in the light of later studies). On the side of *inputs* the pioneer study was by Raymond H. Ewell of the National Science Foundation, who examined research and development (R&D) investments made in the United States during the period from the foundation's inception in 1776 to 1954 (a space of 178 years). Ewell showed in detail that R&D expenditures in the United States have grown at 10 percent *per annum* at least since the first decade of this century, and probably longer. (He also concluded that *half* of the total R&D expenditure of some 40 billion dollars to 1954 had been incurred during the six years from 1948 to 1954.) For a brief description of this work see Raymond H. Ewell, "The Role of Research in Economic Growth," *Chemical and Engineering News,* vol. 33 (1955), pp. 2980–2985. The exponential growth of science (in terms of publications, manpower, findings) also provides one of the basic premises of Pierre Auger's 1960 UNESCO study on *Current Trends in Scientific Research* (Paris and New York: UNESCO Publications, 1961), see especially p. 15.

Overall, Derek J. Price has devoted much effort to the compilation and depiction of the relevant facts, and this chapter has drawn on his discussion. His initial publication in the area was extended in a later paper titled "The Exponential Curve of Science," *Discovery,* 17 (1956), pp. 240–243, and amplified in his books *Science since Babylon* (New Haven: Yale University Press, 1961), and *Little Science, Big Science* (New York: Columbia University Press, 1963). See also Bentley Glass, *The Timely and the Timeless* (New York: Putnam, 1970) as well as Rescher, *Scientific Progress* (Oxford: Blackwell, 1978).

6

Quality Retardation

(1) The issue of importance is obviously a crucial factor for the utilization of information. (2) This, however, is something subject to decidedly different degrees, ranging from the pedestrianly routine to the uncontestably first-rate. (3) The phenomenon of quality retardation so functions that as our information grows, the rate of growth at increasingly higher quality is ever diminished. (4) Higher quality elites are not just increasingly exclusive but slower growing as well. (5) The quality of information is reflected in the structural constitution of texts and in the taxonomies that such structural divisions reflect. (6) In approximation, at least, importance can also be assessed in terms of citations that reflect the utilization of texts in the literature of their subject.

The Centrality of Importance

The previous discussion has conceived of knowledge in terms of top quality, first-rate information. But this is something of an oversimplification. For in cognitive matters, our questions and answers, problems and findings, come in various sizes – some virtually trivial, others portentous, and many somewhere in between. And the difference matters a great deal here. For it is the biggies that figure prominently in textbooks and histories, while the smallies get a footnote at best and blank omission for the most part. Prizes, recognition, and career advancement reward the big, while indifference befalls the small.

In much of the recent period, the pool of information workers has grown rapidly (some 5 percent annually), and their output even more so (an increase of around 15 percent yearly during the twentieth century) indicating an impressively growing efficiency in the production of information.[1] However, what matters in scientific inquiry is progress, and this is determined not through the merely numerical proliferation of findings but through their size – not their mere quantity but the magnitude of their importance in the larger scheme of things. Without the distinction between the important and the unimportant, mankind could neither adequately understand, successfully teach, or effectively practice science.

Importance is a *comparative* conception: one thing is more important than another. And perhaps the most critical fact about cognitive importance is that it is an index of quality – of comparative significance in the context of understanding. It is precisely because one finding is more important than another that it claims and deserves a larger amount of attention and respect. Accordingly, importance is an inherently elitist conception: there is nothing democratic about it.

One key consideration is that being cognitively important is different from being interesting. Interest is subjective; it is dependent on what people happen to be interested in, on what they find interesting. By contrast, cognitive, and in particular scientific, importance is a matter of how prominent a role a fact or finding deserves and thereby demands in an adequate exposition of an area of inquiry. Importance does – or should – function in a way that is objective and impersonal.

Importance in general is a *teleological* conception that connects people with purposes. Something is important *to* someone *for* something, even as eating a good diet is important *to* people-in-general *for* the maintenance of their health. Now what will concern us here is specifically cognitive and in particular scientific importance in the sense not of the importance *of* science for something else (such as human well-being) but rather importance *in* science. What is at issue here is thus the importance *to* serious inquirers *for* the proper understanding of nature's ways.

People have comparatively little difficulty in telling what is *important*, but saying what *importance* is is another matter. Importance is like

---

[1] See M. V. Parat, *The Information Economy: Definition and Measurement* (Washington, DC: U.S. Department of Commerce, May 1977; OT Special Publication 77–12 (1) p. 133. See also Derek J. Price, *Little Science, Big Science* (New York: Columbia University Press, 1963).

pornography – we can generally spot it when we see it all right; it's the matter of adequate definitions and standards that is the difficulty. And so, given the inherent significance of the issue, it is surprising how little literature there is on the topic. I have been able to find only one philosophical handbook or encyclopedia that has an entry under the heading of *importance* – namely, the Spanish encyclopedia of José Ferrater Mora. Its entry is brief and I cite it in full:

Importance: see *relevance*.

But this is clearly not very helpful.

One of the few contemporary philosophers of science who has discussed the topic is Larry Laudan in *Progress and Its Problems*.[2] He observes, "The literature of the methodology of science offers us neither a taxonomy of its types of scientific problems, nor any acceptable method of grounding their relative importance" (p. 13). But Laudan's own discussion is better at diagnosis than therapy: it offers us various examples of important problems, but no effective criteria for what constitutes this virtue. In essence, Laudan sees problems as important to the extent that currently fashionable theories disagree about them. Unfortunately, this idea shipwrecks on the circumstance that theories can disagree about smaller issues as well as large ones.

Perhaps the most promising approach is to see importance as hinging on the answer to the following question: "How large a loss by way of emptiness and unknowing would be created for our grasp of a certain domain if we lost our grip on the information at issue?" So regarded, cognitive importance consists in making a difference for adequate understanding. It is a matter of how large a gap would be left in the body of our presumed knowledge by losing the item at issue. And on this basis it seems plausible at least in the first instance to assess importance in volumetric terms of space allocation in the relevant expositions. Let us consider what can be done along these lines.

Levels of Cognitive Importance

The deliberations of the preceding chapters have been predicated on construing knowledge as elite information, viewing this as subject to

---

[2] Larry Laudan, *Progress and Its Problems* (Berkeley: University of California Press, 1971).

When λ equals	THEN	The quality level of the information at issue is
1		routine $(= I)$
$\frac{1}{4}$		significant
$\frac{1}{2}$		important

DISPLAY 6.1. Levels of informative quality. *Note:* Here quality and quantity are related by the equation: $\#K_\lambda[I] = (\#I)^\lambda$.

a standard which, at the quantitative level, measures the amount of actual knowledge ($\#K$) encompassed in a body of information (I) as standing quantitatively merely at the logarithm thereof: $\#K[I] = \log \#I$. But how does this situation alter if we lower the standard for "knowledge" from the austere condition of first-rate, premium information to something less demanding? How is one to deal in quantitative terms with the lesser levels of "knowledge"?

The obvious response is that "knowledge" then becomes something easier to come by and that with this relaxation a great deal more information will qualify for this honorific designation. Again, a promising way of viewing this matter is to approach it from a quantitative perspective. On this basis, we can now contemplate a spectrum of quality levels whose makeup has the character depicted in Display 6.1 and whose quantitative content is such that

$$\#K_\lambda[I] = (\#I)^\lambda \text{ where } 0 < \lambda \leq 1.$$

Here $K_\lambda[I]$ is the information – or as we can now say, lower-grade "knowledge" – at the quality level λ that is available within the overall body of information I. And this is to be subject to the just-presented stipulation of $\#K_\lambda(I)$ (with the further specification that $\#K_0[I] = \log \#I$).

Thus as conceived here, importance or significance is decidedly *not* a matter of mere proportionality as per "the top 10 percent," or "the leading quarter," or the like. The relationship at issue is *not $\#S_\lambda(I) = \lambda \times 100I$*. This sort of *percent elitism* is not at issue. For while percent elitism is indeed a concept in the economics of money, the economics of information require a more rigorous standard to do justice to the way the concept of importance works in this domain where quality does not keep step with quantity. With cognitive importance we have

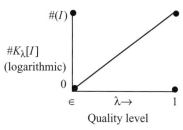

DISPLAY 6.2. The fundamental principle of quality.

to operate the more rigorous standard of a *root elitism* where $\#K_\lambda(I)$ stands as the λ-root of $\#I$: $\#K_\lambda(I) = (\#I)^\lambda$.

This of course means that as I grows (exponentially) over time our "knowledge" at all of the lesser levels of generality will also grow (exponentially), yet doing so at a rate that constantly decreases as the quality level is raised by decreasing λ.

On this basis we arrive at what may be termed the Fundamental Principle of Quality, namely, that since $\log \#K_\lambda[I] = \lambda \log (\#I)$, with a fixed body of information I, the number of items at a given quality level is simply proportionate to the logarithm of the number of items at that quality level. Display 6.2 presents this linear relationship graphically.

Three quality levels are particularly important here. First there is the $\lambda = 1$ level of routine information whose magnitude is that of I itself, namely $\#I$. This may be taken to be measured by the bulk volume of the literature of the field.

A second characteristic level of importance is that afforded by our now familiar standard of paramount quality, "first-rate" information with $\lambda = 1$. Here we have Gibbon's Law: $\#K(I) = \log (\#I)$.

A third level of importance is rooted in the suggestion of Jean Jacques Rousseau[3] that the number of really important items within a population stands as its square root. Here we have $\lambda = \frac{1}{2}$ with the following result:

Number of important items $= \sqrt{\text{total number of items}}$.

---

[3] "Rousseau curiously enough, argued that the size of the [political] elite (i.e., government) varied with the square root of the population, if I understand correctly. This statement that is so frequently imputed to J. J. Rousseau seems to evade specific reference although its sense is apparent in his *Contrat Social*" (George K. Zipf, *Human Behaviour and the Principle of Least Effort* [Boston: Addison-Wesley, 1949], p. 452 & n.).

And there is good reason to think that this is how matters stand in many contexts.[4] Thus, for example, Francis Galton found that at a time when the adult male population of England was some 9,000,000, there were about 3,000 really eminent individuals (persons qualifying as noteworthy by a variety of criteria on the order of featuring in the obituary notices of the *Times*). Also, the square root of the population of a country – or of a profession or other category – yields (to within a reasonable approximation) the number of listings in a head count of the top elite for the constituency at issue.[5] Or, there are in the United States roughly 1,600 educational institutions that grant a baccalaureate degree, but only some $40(=\sqrt{1,600})$ of them comprise the really "major universities," which produce three-quarters of the Ph.D.s and the vast majority of scholarly books and papers.

These observations situate three particularly significant levels of informative quality within the overall spectrum presented in Display 6.1.

On the basis of these considerations, quality can be assessed straight-forwardly in terms of quantity: more is less. But of course what is at issue here is not so much a discovery about quality as a definition of those K_λ-quality levels. In putting a number to the volume of high-quality findings, the question remains: which is the dependent and which the independent variable? Do we have standards first and then numbers or the other way round? And here our present approach is essentially that of the second alternative.

Quality Retardation

It is obvious that information of high quality will always be less in quantity than information at large. But what is far from obvious – and perhaps surprising – is that *the growth of high-quality information is not proportional to that of information at large, but is distinctly slower; moreover, this rate of growth decelerates as the bar of qualification at issue with "high quality" is raised.* This quantitative slowing of growth in the wake of

---

[4] Derek J. Price, *Little Science, Big Science* (New York: Columbia University Press, 1963), pp. 33–36, provides a sketch of Galton's findings.

[5] However, the 2003–04 *Who's Who in America* lists 79,000 individuals at a time when the population of the country stands at some 280 million (with a square root of ca. 5,300). This exaggeration by a factor of 15 the Rousseau's law standard is typical of national *Who's Whos*. No doubt, the editors of such works are inclined for commercial reasons to exaggerate who is a who.

Quality level (K_λ)	Cumulative number of items of at least that level	Doubling time	Per annum growth rate
$\lambda = 1$: "routine"	$I = I'$	15 years	5%
$\lambda = .75$: "significant"	$I^{.75}$	20 years	2.75%
$\lambda = .5$: "important"	$I^{.5} = \sqrt{I}$	30 years	2.5%

DISPLAY 6.3. The principle of quality retardation: The decreasing rate growth of scientific information at increasing quality levels. *Note:* This relation between quantity and quality is predicated on taking *I* as the scientific literature at large which has been growing at a doubling time of some 15 years throughout the modern era.

qualitative escalation may be characterized as *quality retardation.* The structure of its phenomenology is exhibited in Display 6.3.[6]

There are many illustrations of this phenomenon. For instance, during the 20th century, memberships in the American Physical Society grew from some 100 in 1900 to over 40,000 in 2000, doubling roughly every 12 years. The fellows of the society who represent its more distinguished, elite members, while also increasing in numbers, represented 100 percent of its membership in the early years but only one-eighth thereof at the end of the century. Then too, while the literature in genetics has increased exponentially during the twentieth century with a doubling time of some 15 years, the "significant discoveries" in the field as inventoried by Bentley Glass has merely increased, with a doubling time of some 20 years.[7]

On this basis, it is a significant lesson of the Principle of Quality Retardation that the increase of significant information lags substantially behind the increase of information at large. Given an information manifold *I*, the basic relation $\#K_\lambda[I] = (\#I)^\lambda$ leads straightforwardly to

$$\#K_\lambda[2 \times I] = \#(2 \times I)^2 = K_\lambda[I] \times 2^\lambda.$$

[6] On the general situation see the author's *Scientific Progress* (Oxford: Basil Blackwell, 1978), especially Chapter 6, "The Quantity of Quantity," pp. 95–111. For the empirical substantiation of this effect see Roland Wagner–Döbler, "Rescher's Principle of Decreasing Marginal Returns for Scientific Research," *Scientometrics*, 50 (2001), pp. 419–36.

[7] Bentley Glass, "Milestones and Rates of Growth in the Development of Biology," *Quarterly Review of Biology*, 54 (March 1979), pp. 31–53.

Thus, with information at the $\lambda = \frac{1}{2}$ level of "importance, we have $K_{\frac{1}{2}}[2 \times I] = \sqrt{2} \times K_{\frac{1}{2}}[I]$. In doubling the information we have increased its informativity important component by a factor of only $\sqrt{2} \cong 1.41$, so that in doubling information we have amplified our "knowledge" not by another unit of 1 but merely by 0.41. And the further step to $3I$ would carry us further by only 0.32. We thus encounter an instance of the generic situation that the amplification of information is subject to diminishing cognitive returns. Within any given course of congnitive growth, the *rate* of progress decreases drastically as one raises the standard of quality: the higher one sets the bar, the slower the advance.

Elites

All of the standards of the "knowledge" at issue with quality information, with $\lambda > 0$ are elitist in a manner suggestive of "lion's share" possession. We often hear that the richest 5 percent of the American population owns 70 percent of the nation's privately held wealth; or again, that the top 25 percent of university libraries account for 50 percent of all university library holdings in the United States. In this vein, consider the eliteness function defined by the following condition:

$E(x) = y$ iff $x\%$ of the overall population at issue accounts for $y\%$ of the whole of some parameter.

Let us define the "haves" subgroup of a population as the one that accounts for 50 percent of the whole "ownership" of the parametric quantity at issue. With a "fair" deliberation, the haves will be just as numerous as the have-nots. However, with what we shall call an "elitist" distribution, this relationship functions like the curve of Display 6.4. As this representation indicates, with an elitist distribution a comparatively small proportion of the population will have a lion's share of the whole.

A vivid illustration of this phenomenon is "Lotka's Law" to the effect that if k is the number of scientists who publish just one paper, then the number publishing n papers is k/n^2. In many branches of science this works out to some 5–6 percent of scientists producing half of all papers in their discipline, putting the subgroup of the haves at about one-twentieth of the whole.[8]

---

[8] On Lotka's Law see Derek Price, *Science since Babylon* (New Haven: Yale University Press, 1961; 2nd ed. 1975), pp. 174–75. For further information see Paul A. David,

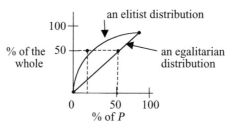

DISPLAY 6.4. An elitist distribution. *Note: The straight line represents a perfect egalitarianism, while the curve represents an elitist distribution of sorts.*

$$E_0 = P, \text{ the overall population}$$

$$E_1 = 10\% \text{ of } E_0 = .1 \times P$$

$$E_2 = 10\% \text{ of } E_1 = .01 \times P$$

$$E_i = 10\% \text{ of } E_{2-1} = (.1)^i \times P$$

DISPLAY 6.5. Nested n-th order proportionality elites.

In this regard, the idea of rank importance paves the way to what may be called the Proportional Law of Elites. The guiding idea here is that the comparative size of an elite (at a certain level of exclusivity) is to be determined by a specified proportion or percentage of the population at issue. Thus with an overall population of size P and an elitism proportion of 10 percent we would have the sizes for the nested sequence of successively higher, "more exclusive" elites given in Display 6.5. Here every step onward in the eliteness sequence reduces the group at issue by an order of magnitude. And this is only to be expected since diminished quantity and increased quality go hand in hand.

The situation depicted in Display 6.5 leads to the Proportional Law of Elites (as we shall call it), which specifies the overall size of successively "exclusive" elites. In general, with a population of size P there will be a series of $\log P$ one-tenth proportionality eliteness levels, with each such level E_i containing $(.1)^i \times P$ members. Overall, elitist hierarchies are by nature reflective of an exponential decay. (An army will always have far fewer generals than privates.) And with any elitist

"Positive Feedback and Research Productivity in Science," in O. Granstrand (ed.), *The Economics of Technology* (Amsterdam: Elsevier, 1994), pp. 65–89.

distribution of a good in the manner of Display 6.4, an E_i-elite rather far down the line in Display 6.5 will manage to comprise all the "haves" there are. Thus in scientific publications, for example, some 10 percent of the articles will engross 50 percent of citation references, so that the E_1 elite effectively constitutes the "haves" in point of professional recognition.[9]

Cognitive Importance as Reflected in Space Allocation

What form will the idealized systematization of a body of knowledge take? A promising answer is that it is a matter of "perfected textbooks" – ideally perfected systemic accounts. After all, information gets organized through textual exposition – for simplicity let us say by getting put into print in books. And cognitive systems so construed are encompassed in (usually) well-formed and cogently organized symbolically presented expositions which, in their turn, yield libraries, library sections, books, and then out to chapters, sections, and so on.

To illustrate this approach to systemic structuring of cognition, let's begin with a relevantly structured unit such as a scientific/technical book or monograph along by now thoroughly familiar lines. Such a treatise will of course be divided into chapters, sections, paragraphs, and sentences, and for the sake of discussion, we may suppose a situation of the type sketched in Display 6.6. The result will be a more or less standard modest-size book of some $10^5 = 100,000$ words or 250 pages. And of course a complex topic will require many such volumes.

On this basis, it is instructive to look at the matter of importance from the angle of the allocation of space in a well-designed articulation of the issues. For an ideal exposition space allocation in expository matters would of course reflect the importance of the matters involved. And on this basis the importance of a cognitive unit such as an idea or thesis or line of thought can be measured by the magnitude (book or chapter or section) of the space devoted to it in an adequate exposition of its domain. And, of course, our book analogy could be replicated on a larger scale in such a sequence as cognitive domain, discipline, substantive, specialty, problem area, problem, problem component. Accordingly, if space – and thus, effectively, attention – is seen as

[9] See H. W. Holub, G. Tappeiner, and V. Eberharter, "The Iron Law of Important Articles," *Southern Economic Journal*, 58 (1991), pp. 317–28.

1 book $\sim$ 100%	(level 1)
1 chapter $\sim$ 10%	(level 2)
1 section $\sim$ 1%	(level 3)
1 paragraph $\sim$ .1%	(level 4)
1 sentence $\sim$ .01%	(level 5)

DISPLAY 6.6. Space allocation for a hypothetical treatise. *Note:* In general, one level n unit merits a space allocation proportional to $\frac{1000\%}{10^n} = 10^{n-3}\%$. On this basis we have log $Sn \propto n$: the logarithm of the space allocated is an effective index of importance levels.

Q_0 1 big (first importance) idea for the book-as-a-whole.

Q_1 10 sizeable (second importance) idea: one for each chapter.

Q_2 100 moderately (third importance) idea: one for each section.

Q_3 1,000 smallish (fourth importance) idea: one for each paragraph.

DISPLAY 6.7. Quality levels. *Note:* In general, $Q_i = 10^i$ or equivalently log $Q_i \propto i$.

importance-reflective, then we will have the upshot that our illustrative book affords us ideas or findings at the level of magnitude indicated in Display 6.7. As this relationship of quality and quantity suggests, quality varies with the inverse of quantity, or put differently, eliteness and quantity stand in a relationship of complimentarity.

Let's suppose the organizational taxonomy structure of a book is indicated by its table of contents – and the structure of a body of texts by their taxonomic inventory. The comparative importance is represented by taxonomic depth (or rather, shallowness). So here structure reflects significance. The further down an item figures on the list of cumulating chapters, sections, or paragraphs, the lower the grade of its importance becomes.

We thus arrive at what might be characterized as *the ideal space-allocation standard of importance.* A scientific idea, concept, principle, thesis, theory, finding, or fact is important exactly to the comparative extent to which it merits space allocation in a perfected exposition of its field.

So importance is plausibly viewed *in the light of the idea of a perfected textbook for the domain at issue.* And importance will here be reflected in space allocation. To reemphasize: the crucial determinative factor for increasing importance is the extent of seismic disturbance of the cognitive terrain. Without the idea or concept of issue, would we have to abandon and/or rewrite the entire textbook, or a whole chapter, or a section, or a paragraph, or a sentence, or a mere footnote?

This, of course, puts the issue in the light of idealization. But we can also look to the real and thus implement the distinction between putative and actual importance. And here as elsewhere the actual may be seen as affording at least an *approximation* of the ideal.

Importance is thus seen as reflected in a Perfected Scientific Library when each domain of factual knowledge would be given its canonically definitive systematization – its perfected account in terms of correctness and completeness.[10] However to implement this idea we must deal with the reality of actual science libraries in place of that idealization. We must, in short, take the Hegelian line that the real is rational, and that the reality of things stands for that otherwise unattainable idealization.

This being so, it should be clear that when we ourselves actually engage in the business of attributing importance to facts and findings we are providing *estimates* of importance. Importance for science as we have it here-and-now is one sort of thing – namely, putative or estimated and thus subjective importance – while real, objective importance is a matter of how matters stand in ideal or perfected science. But given that *science-as-best-we-can-devise-it* is more or less by definition our best available *estimate* of *science as it would ideally be developed,* the two can be viewed in practice as representing different sides of the same coin.

Cognitive Importance as Reflected in Citation

In relation to *particular* members of a population we can adopt the following principle:

The importance ranking of a particular item is to be assessed by the index of the smallest (most restrictive) elite to which it belongs.

[10] This model of a Perfected Library is – to be sure – something very different from the Borges Library contemplated by the Argentinean polymath Jorge Luis Borges. For the Borges Library is universal: it deals not only with actuality but seeks to map out the realm of possibility as well. Accordingly, the vast bulk of its holdings will be works of fiction rather than of science. Our presently envisioned Perfected Scientific Library, by contrast, concerns itself with fact alone, and leaves fiction aside.

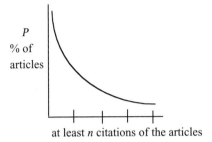

DISPLAY 6.8. The citation distribution of articles. *Note:* In effect, we have a pattern of exponential decay.

On this basis, the importance of rank-ordered items of any sort is proportional to the logarithm of the sum total of at least equally important items – a principle we have already seen at work with respect to knowledge. The key to the quality-quantity relationship at issue here is provided by the work of George K. Zipf. His classic book, *Human Behaviour and the Principle of Least Effort*,[11] insisted that in a wide variety of circumstances the situation of Display 6.8 prevails. The relationship set out here is linked to an equilateral hyperbola of the format $s \times \log (\#s) =$ const. On this basis we can look at the situation in light of the Fundamental Principle of Quality discussed in relation to Display 6.2 above, which in effect says measure quality by the logarithm of quantity.

Scientific importance is not a qualitative but a relational feature, a function of how one item (fact or idea, etc.) relates to the others. Specifically, when something is important, a lot else depends on its being the way it is, and this is bound to be reflected in how much occasion there is to have recourse to it in an adequate systematization of the domain at issue. This approach inflects a fundamentally pragmatic perspective. It views cognitive objects such as concepts, ideas, and theories as *tools*. And with any sort of production process – be it physical or cognitive – the importance of a tool lies in how much occasion one has to make use of it.

And here issues of citation frequency and space allocation come in. For starters, throughout scientific publication (as numerous structures indicate), the logarithm of the number of papers cited n times graphs

---

[11] Boston: Addison-Wesley, 1949.

Quality level (K_λ)	λ-value	n-value (for E_n)	Percentage of papers of at least this level
			(at a 50% reduction per level)
Routine	1	0	100
Significant	.75	1	50
Important	.5	2	25
Very important	.25	3	12.5

DISPLAY 6.9. The quantity of quality.

linearly against *n*, so it transpires that we can also use citation frequency as a measure of quality. As a rough approximation, the fraction of the number of papers in a scientific field, the number that will be cited *n* times, is given by $\frac{1}{2}, \frac{1}{4}, \frac{1}{8}, \cdots (\frac{1}{2})^n \ldots$ respectively as *n* = 1, 2, 3, 4, ... This means that the percentage of papers that will be cited exactly *n* times will stand at 50, 25, 12.5, 6.2, ... respectively as *n* = 1, 2, 3, 4, ... The statistics of the situation invite us to associate citation frequencies with the quality levels of Display 6.1 above, and on this basis we obtain the situation of Display 6.9.[12]

These considerations provide another convenient bridge to the qualification of knowledge. Setting out from the idea of a citation network, we can assess the size of an item by the extent of its enmeshment – the number of citation linkages with others. Now in view of Zipf's findings,

The importance-reflective size of an item (in terms of the number of its linkages) is inversely proportional to the number of items of at least that quality.

But from the analysis of elites it emerges that

The quality of an item is inversely proportional to the logarithm of a number of items of at least that quality.

On this basis we can conclude that

The quality of an item is proportionate to (and can thus be measured in terms of) the number of its citation linkages.

[12] For the empirical substantiation of this general pattern see the already cited publications of Derek Price as well as William Shockley, "On the Statistics of Productivity in Research," *Proceedings of the Institute of Radio Engineeers*, 45 (1957), pp. 279–90, and William Goffin and Kenneth S. Warren, *Scientific Information Systems and the Principle of Solidarity* (New York: Praeger, 1981).

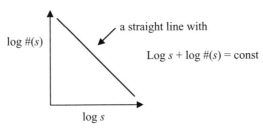

DISPLAY 6.10. Zipf's law of rank order. *Note:* s = the size of an object $\#(s)$ = the object's place in the rank-order of size.

We thus arrive at the conclusion that the analysis of citation linkages affords a suitable way of assessing the cognitive quality of individual items of information. And given that "knowledge" (in its various degrees) is a matter of the quality of the information at issue, this serves to indicate the utility of citation analysis in measuring knowledge.

But now another line of consideration enters in. Many studies of citation statistics confirm the picture of Display 6.10 as holding throughout science and its branches.[13] The same drastic picture of exponential decline in point of quantity obtains on both sides. And so the lesson is clear: importance can just as effectively be estimated in terms of prominence in citation space as by prominence in discussion space.

And so, to whatever extent we are prepared to see the actual space allocations as an approximation of the ideal situation, we can undertake the shift from seeming to actual importance.

[13] A starting point is provided by the books of Derek J. Price, *Science since Babylon* (New Haven: Yale University Press, 1975), and *Little Science, Big Science* (New York: Columbia University Press, 1963). An updated source is H. W. Holub, Gottfried Tappeiner, and Veronica Eberharter, "The Iron Law of Important Articles," *Southern Economic Journal,* 58 (1991), pp. 317–28. The journal *Scientometrics* has published a great deal of relevant material in recent years.

7

How Much Can Be Known?

A Leibnizian Perspective on the Quantitative Discrepancy Between Linguistic Truth and Objective Fact

(1) Propositional knowledge is a matter of textualization that hinges on linguistic realizability. (2) As Leibniz realized, this imposes limits. (3)–(6) While statements (and thus truths and realizable knowledge) are enumerable, actual objective facts are not, for there is good reason to think that facts are inexhaustible and nondenumerable. (7) Accordingly, there are more facts than truths: reality bursts the bounds of textualization. (8)–(9) There are various facts that we finite beings cannot manage to know. (10)–(11) There is no warrant for the view that reality as such answers to what we can know of it.

How Much Can a Person Know? Leibniz on Language Combinatorics

Gibbon's Law holds that the extraction of knowledge from mere information becomes exponentially more demanding in the course of cognitive progress. However, while finite resources will doubtless impose limits in practice, the process is one which in theory and principle goes endlessly on and on. Does this mean that there really are no theoretical limits to the enlargement of knowledge?

To this point, the book's deliberations have dealt with knowledge in relation to what people know. But above and beyond what is *known* there is also the issue of what is *knowable.*

How much can someone possibly know? What could reasonably be viewed as an upper limit to an individual's knowledge – supposing that factually informative knowledge rather than performative how-to knowledge or subliminally tacit knowledge is at issue?

73

In pursuing this question, it is convenient to continue along the lines of our textual approach. Accordingly, let us suppose someone with perfect recall who devotes a long life span to the acquisition of information. For 70 years this individual spends 365 days per annum reading for 12 hours a day at the rate of 60 pages an hour (with 400 words per page). That yields a lifetime reading quota of some 7.4×10^9 words. Optimistically supposing that, on average, a truth regarding some matter of fact or other takes only some seven words to state, this means a lifetime access to some 10^9 truths, around a billion of them: 1,000,000,000. No doubt most of us are a great deal less well informed than this. But it seems pretty well acceptable as an upper limit for the information that a human individual could probably not reach and certainly not exceed.

After all, with an average of 400 pages per book, the previously indicated lifetime reading quota would come to some 46,000 books. The world's largest libraries – the Library of Congress, for example – currently have somewhere around 20 million books (book-length assemblages of monographs and pamphlets included). And it would take a very Hercules of reading to make his way through even one-quarter of 1 percent of so vast a collection (= 50,000), which is roughly what our aforementioned reading prodigy manages. So while a given individual can read *any* book (there are no inherently *unreadable* books), the individual cannot possibly read *every* book (for any one of us there are bound to be very many *unread* books indeed). If mastery of Library of Congress-encompassed material is to be the measure, then few of us would be able to hold our heads up very high.[1]

All this, of course, still only addresses the question of how much knowledge a given person – one particular individual – can manage to acquire. There yet remains the question of how much is in principle knowable – that is, *can be known*. And here it is instructive to begin

---

[1] To be sure, there lurks in the background the question of whether having mere *information* is to count as having *knowledge*. With regard to this quantitative issue it has been argued here that authentic knowledge does not increase propositionally with the amount of information as such, but only proportionally with its logarithm. This would suggest that the actual knowledge within the Library of Congress's many volumes could be encompassed telegraphically in some far more modest collection, so that our Herculean reader could access about half of the actual knowledge afforded by the LC's vast collection.

with the perspective of the great 17th-century polymath G. W. Leibniz (1646–1717).

Leibniz took his inspiration from *The Sand Reckoner* of Archimedes, who sought to determine the astronomically large number of sand grains that could be contained within the universe defined by the sphere of the fixed stars of Aristotelian cosmology – a number Archimedes effectively estimated at 10^{50}. Thus even as Archimedes addressed the issue of the scope of *the physical universe*, so Leibniz sought to address the issue of the scope of *the universe of thought*.[2] For just this is what he proceeded to do in a fascinating 1693 tract *On the Horizon of Human Knowledge* (*De l'horizon de la doctrine humaine*).[3]

Leibniz pursued this project very much in the spirit of the preceding ideas. He wrote:

All items of human knowledge can be expressed by the letters of the alphabet...so that it follows that one can calculate the number of truths of which humans are capable and thus compute the size of a work that would contain all possible human knowledge, and which would contain all that could ever be known, written, or invented, and more besides. For it would contain not only the truths, but also all the falsehoods that men can assert, and meaningless expressions as well.[4]

Thus if one could set an upper limit to the volume of printed matter accessible to inquiring humans, then one could map out by combinatorial means the whole manifold of accessible verbal material – true, false, or gibberish – in just the manner that Leibniz contemplated.

Any alphabet devisable by man will have only a limited number of letters (Leibniz here supposes the Latin alphabet of 24 which takes *w* and *W*). So even if we allow a word to become very long indeed

---

[2] On Archimedes' estimate see T. C. Heath, *The Works of Archimedes* (Cambridge: Cambridge University Press, 1897).

[3] See G. W. Leibniz, *De l'horizon de la doctrine humaine*, ed. by Michael Fichant (Paris: Vrin, 1991). There is a partial translation of Leibniz's text in "Leibniz on the Limits of Human Knowledge," by Philip Beeley, *The Leibniz Review*, 13 (December 2003), pp. 93–97. (Note that in old French "doctrine" means *knowledge*.) It is well known that Leibniz invented entire branches of science, among the differential and integral calculatus, the calculus of variations, topology (analysis situs), symbolic logic, and computers. But he deserves to be seen as a pioneer of epistemetrics as well. The relevant issues are analyzed in Nicholas Rescher, "Leibniz's Quantitative Epistemology," *Studia Leibnitiana*, (in press).

[4] Leibniz, *De l'horizon*, pp. 37–38.

(Leibniz overgenerously supposes 32 letters)[5] there will be only a limited number of words that can possibly be formed (namely 24 exp 32). And so, if we suppose a maximum to the number of words that a single run-on, just barely intelligible sentence can contain (say 100), then there will be a limit to the number of potential "statements" that can possibly be made, namely 100 exp (24 exp 32).[6] This number is huge indeed – far bigger than Archimedes' sand grains. Nevertheless, it is still finite, limited. Moreover, with an array of basic symbols different from those of the Latin alphabet, the situation is changed in detail but not in structure. (And this remains the case even if one adds the symbols at work in mathematics, and here Leibniz was thinking of Descartes's translation of geometrically pictorial propositions into an algebraically articulated format as well as his own project of a universal language and a *calculus ratiocinator*.)[7]

The crux of Leibniz's discussion is that any fact that can be framed in a proposition can in principle be spelled out in print. And there is only so much, so *finitely* much, that can be stated in sentences of intelligible length – and therefore only so much that can explicitly be thought by beings who conduct their thinking in language. Moreover, because this speculation encompasses fiction as well, our knowledge of possibility is also finite, and fiction is for us just as much language-limited as is the domain of truth.

---

[5] The longest word I have seen in actual use is the 34-letter absurdity *supercalifragilistic-expialidocious* from the musical *Mary Poppins*.

[6] G. W. Leibniz, *De l'horizon*, p. 11. This of course long antedates the (possibly apocryphal) story about the Huxley-Wilberforce debate, which has Huxley arguing that sensible meaning could result from chance process because a team of monkeys typing at random would eventually produce the works of Shakespeare – or (on some account) all the books in the British Library, including not only Shakespeare's works but the Bible as well. (The story – also found in Sir Arthur Eddington's *The Nature of the Physical World* [London: McMillan, 1929], pp. 72–73 – is doubtless fictitious since the Huxley-Wilberforce debate of 1860 antedated the emergence of the typewriter.) However, the basic idea goes back at least to Cicero: "If a countless number of the twenty-one letters of the alphabet...were mixed together it is possible that when cast on the ground they should make up the *Annals* of Ennius, able to be read in good order" (*De natura deorum*, II, 27). The story launched an immense discussion that continues actively on the contemporary scene as is readily attested by a Google or Yahoo search for "typing monkeys." It has also had significant literary repercussions as is exemplified by Jorge Luis Borges's well-known story of "The Library of Babel," which contains all possible books.

[7] Louis Couturat, *La logique de Leibniz* (Paris: Alcan, 1901) is still the best overall account of this Leibnizian project.

The Leibnizian Perspective

The moment one sets a realistic limit to the length of practicably mean-ingful sentences one has to realize that the volume of the sayable is finite – vast though it will be. And this means that as long as people transact their thinking in language – broadly understood to encom-pass the whole diversity of symbolic devices – the thoughts they can have, and thereby the things they possibly can know, will be limited in number.

Moving further along these lines, the *cognitive* (in contrast to the *affective*) thought-life of people consists of the language-framed propo-sitions they consider. And let us suppose that people can consider tex-tualized propositions at about the same speed at which they can read – optimistically, some 60 pages per hour with each page consisting of 20 sentences. Assuming a thought-span of 16 waking hours on average, in the course of a year a person can entertain a number of propositional thoughts equal to

$$365 \times 16 \times 60 \times 20 \cong 7 \times 10^6.$$

So, subject to the hypotheses at issue, this is how much material one would need if he were to replicate in print the stream of consciousness thought–life of a person for an entire year. Once again, this number of seven million, though not small, is nevertheless limited. And these limits will again finitize the combinatorial possibilities. A person can manage only so much thinking. And in the context of a finite species, these limits of language mean that there are only so many thoughts to go around – only so many manageable sentences to be formulated. Once again we are in the grip of finitude.

Now as Leibniz saw it, matters can be carried much further. For the finitude at issue here has highly significant implications. Con-sider an analogy. Only a finite number of hairs will fit on a person's head – say 1,000. So when there are enough individuals in a group (say 1,001 of them) then two of them must have exactly the same num-ber of hairs on their heads. And so also with thoughts. Even as laws have to fit within the available dermatology, so they will have to fit within the available textuality. If there are sufficiently many thinking intelligences in the aeons of cosmic history while yet the number of thoughts – and thus also thought-days and thought-lives – are finite, then there will inevitably be several people in a sufficiently large linguistic community whose thoughts are precisely the same throughout their lives.

It also becomes a real prospect that language imposes limits on our grasp of people and their doings. Thus suppose that the Detailed Biography of a person is a minute-by-minute account of his or her doings, allocating (say) 10 printed lines to each minute, and so roughly 15,000 lines per day to make up a hefty volume of 300 fifty-line pages. If a paradigmatic individual lives 100 years we will need 365×100 or roughly 36,500 such substantial tomes to provide a comprehensive step-by-step account of his or her life.

But, as we have seen, the number of such tomes, though vast, is limited. In consequence, there are only so many Detailed Biographies to go around, so the number of Detailed Biographies that are available is also finite. This, of course, means that *if the duration of the species were long enough* – or if the vastness of space provided sufficiently many thinkers – *then there would have to be some people with exactly the same Detailed Biography*. Given enough agents, eventual repetitions in point of their doings become inevitable.

And now, moving on from biographies (or diaries) to public annals, Leibniz thought to encounter much the same general situation once again. Suppose that (as Leibniz has it) the world's population is one hundred million (that is 10^8) and that each generation lives (on average) for 50 years. Then in the 6,000 years during which civilized man may be supposed to have existed, there have lived some 1.2×10^{10} people – or some 10^{10} of them if we assume smaller generations in earlier times.[8]

Recall now the above-mentioned idea of 36,500 hefty tomes needed to characterize in detail the life of an individual. It then follows that we would need some 36.5×10^{13} of them for a complete history of the species. To be sure, we thus obtain an astronomically vast number of possible overall annals for mankind as a whole. But though vast, this number will nevertheless be finite. And so, if the history of the race is sufficiently long, then some part of its extensive history will have to repeat itself in full with a *parfaite repetition mot pour mot*, since there are only so many possible accounts of a given day (or week or year).

---

[8] Leibniz, *De l'horizon*, p. 112.

For, once again, there are only a finite number of possibilities to go around, and somewhere along the line total repetitions will transpire and life stories will occasionally recur *in toto* (*ut homines novi eadem ad sensum penitus tota vita agerent, quae alii jam egerunt*).⁹

As Leibniz thus saw it, the finitude of language and its users carries in its wake the finitude of possible diaries, biographies, histories – you name it, including even possible thought-lives in the sense of propositionalized streams of consciousness as well. Even as Einstein with his general relativity (initially) saw himself as finitizing the size of the physical universe, so Leibniz's treatise saw the size of mankind's cognitive universe as a manifold of limited horizons – boundless but finite.

It was accordingly a key aspect of Leibniz's thought that human understanding cannot keep up with reality. For Leibniz, the propositional thought of finite creatures is linguistic and thereby finite and limited. But he also held that reality – as captured in the thought of God, if you will – is infinitely detailed. Only God's thought can encompass it, not ours. Reality's infinite detail thus carries both costs and benefits in its wake. Its cost is the unavoidability of imperfect comprehension by finite intelligences. Its benefit is the prospect of endless variability and averted repetition. And the result is a cognitively insuperable gap between epistemology and metaphysics. Everything that humans can say or think by linguistic means can be comprehended in one vast but finite Universal Library.¹⁰

But what do these Leibnizian ruminations mean in the larger scheme of things?

Twentieth-century philosophers of otherwise the most radically different orientation have agreed on prioritizing the role of language. "The limits of my language set the limits of my world" ("Die Grenzen meiner Spache bedeuten die Grenzen meiner Welt") says the Wittgenstein of the *Tractatus* at 5.6. "There is nothing outside text" ("Il n'y a pas de hors de texte") say the devotees of French deconstructionism. But already centuries earlier Leibniz had taken the measure of this sort of textualism. He looked at it up close and saw that it could not be sustained.

---

⁹ Ibid., p. 54.
¹⁰ This of course leads back to the Borges Library of footnote 10 of Chapter 6.

Statements Are Enumerable, As Are Truths

The preceding deliberations have unfolded on the basis of the emphatically contingent supposition that there are certain limits to human capabilities – and, in particular, to the length of the words and sentences with which our discourse can effectively operate. But let us now also waive this (otherwise surely realistic) restriction and break through the limits of finitude in the interests of getting a grip on the general principles of the matter.

Even if one construes the idea of an "alphabet" sufficiently broadly to include not only letters but symbols of various sorts, it still holds that everything stateable in a language can be spelled out in print through the combinational concatenation of some sequential register of symbols.[11] And with a "language" construed as calling for development in the usual recursive manner, it transpires that the statements of a language can be enumerated in a vast and indeed infinite but nevertheless ultimately countable listing.[12] But since the world's languages, even if not finite in number, are nevertheless at most enumerable, it follows that the set of all statements – including every linguistically formable proposition – will be *enumerably* infinite (and thus have the transfinite cardinality that mathematicians designate as alef-zero).

As a matter of principle, then, we obtain

Thesis 1: *The Enumerability of Statements.* Statements (linguistically formulated propositions) are enumerable and thus (at most) denumerably infinite.

Our linguistic resources for describing concrete states of affairs are thus subject to quantitative limitation. And insofar as our thought about things proceeds by recursively developed linguistic means, it is inherently limited in its reach within the confines of countability. And so the upshot is that the limits of textuality impose quantitative limitations on propositionalized thought – albeit not limits of finitude.

Being inherently linguistic in character, truths are indissolubly bound to textuality, seeing that any language-framed declaration can be generated recursively from a sequential string of symbols – that is,

---

[11] Compare Philip Hugly and Charles Sayward, "Can a Language Have Indenumerably Many Expressions?" *History and Philosophy of Logic,* 4, 1983, pp. 98–117.

[12] This supposes an upper limit to the length of intelligible statements. And even if this restriction were waived, the number of statements will still be no more than *countably* infinite.

that all spoken language can in principle be reduced to writing. Since they correspond to statements, it follows that truths cannot be more than countably infinite. And on this basis we have

Thesis 2: *The Denumerability of Truth.* While the manifold of the truth cannot be finitely inventoried, nevertheless, truths are no more than denumerably infinite in number.

Truths versus Facts

We serve the interests of clarity to introduce a distinction at this stage – that between truths and facts. Truths are linguistically stated facts, correct statements, in sum, which, as such, must be formulated in language (broadly understood to include symbols systems of various sorts). A "truth" is something that has to be framed in *linguistic/symbolic* terms – the representation of a fact through its statement in some language, so that any correct statement represents a truth.

A "fact," on the other hand, is not a linguistic item at all, but an actual aspect of the world's state of affairs and is thereby a feature of reality.[13] Facts correspond to *potential* truths whose actualization as such waits upon their appropriate linguistic embodiment. Truths are statements and thus language bound, but facts outrun linguistic limits. Once stated, a fact yields a truth, but with facts at large there need in principle be no linguistic route to get from here to there.

The Inexhaustibility of Fact

Accordingly, facts need not be exhausted by truths. It is a key facet of our epistemic stance toward the real world that its furnishings possess a complexity and diversity of detail so elaborate that there is *always* more to be said than we have so far managed. Every part and parcel of reality has features beyond the range of our current cognitive reach – at any juncture whatsoever.

Moreover, any adequate account of inquiry must recognize that the process of information acquisition at issue in science is a process of

---

[13] Our position thus takes no issue with P. F. Strawson's precept that "facts are what statements (when true) state." ("Truth," *Proceedings of the Aristotelian Society*, Supplementary Vol. 24, 1950, pp. 129–56; see p. 136.) Difficulty would ensue with Strawson's thesis only if an "only" were added.

conceptual innovation. In consequence, the ongoing progress of scientific inquiry always leaves various facts about the things of this world wholly outside the conceptual realm of the inquirers of any particular period. Caesar did not know – and in the state of the cognitive art of his time could not have known – that his sword contained tungsten and carbon. There will always be facts about a thing that we do not *know* because we cannot even *express* them in the prevailing conceptual order of things. To grasp such a fact means taking a perspective of consideration that as yet we simply do not have, because the state of knowledge (or purported knowledge) has not reached a point at which such a consideration is *feasible*. And so, the facts about any actual physical object – are in theory inexhaustible.

Its susceptibility to further elaborate detail – and to changes of mind regarding this further detail – is built into our very conception of a "real thing." The range of fact about anything real is thus effectively inexhaustible. There is, as best we can tell, no limit to the world's ever-increasing complexity that comes to view with our ever-increasing grasp of its detail. The realm of fact and reality is endlessly variegated and complex. And so we also arrive at

Thesis 3: *The Inexhaustibility of Fact.* Facts are infinite in number. The domain of fact is inexhaustible: there is no limit to facts about the real.

In this regard, however, real things differ in an interesting and important way from fictive ones. For a key about *fictional* particulars is that they are of finite cognitive depth. In characterizing them we shall ultimately run out of steam as regards their nongeneric features. A point will always be reached when one cannot say anything further that is characteristically new about them – presenting nongeneric information that is not inferentially implicit in what has already been said.[14] New *generic* information can, of course, always be forthcoming through the progress of science: when we learn more about coal in general, then we also know more about the coal in Sherlock Holmes's grate. But the finiteness of its cognitive depth means that the prospect

---

[14] To deny inferentially implicit information the title of authentic *novelty*, is not, of course, to say that it cannot *surprise* us in view of the limitations of our own deductive powers.

of ampliatively novel *nongeneric* information must by the very nature of the case come to a stop when fictional things are at issue.

With *real* things, on the other hand, there is no reason of principle why the elaboration of nongenerically idiosyncratic information need ever end. On the contrary, we have every reason to presume real things to be cognitively inexhaustible. The prospect of discovery is open-ended here. A precommitment to description-transcending features – no matter how far description is pushed – is essential to our conception of a real thing.

The detail of the real world is inexhaustible: obtaining fuller information about its constituents is always possible in principle – though not of course in practice, since only a finite number of things have actually been said up to now – or indeed up to any actually realized moment of world history. Something whose character was exhaustible by linguistic characterization would thereby be marked as fictional rather than real.[15]

And so we have it that facts regarding reality are infinite in number. But just how infinite?

Facts Are Transdenumerable

While statements in general – and therefore true statements in particular – can be enumerated, and truths are consequently denumerable in number, there is good reason to suppose that this will not hold for facts. On the contrary, there is every reason to think that, reality being what it is, there will be an uncountably large manifold of facts.

The reality is that facts, unlike truths, cannot be enumerated: *no listing of fact-presenting truths – not even one of infinite length – can possibly manage to constitute a complete register of facts.* Any attempt to register fact-as-a-whole will founder: the list is bound to be incomplete because there are facts about the list-as-a-whole which no single entry can encompass.

---

[15] This also explains why the dispute over mathematical realism (Platonism) has little bearing on the issue of physical realism. Mathematical entities are akin to fictional entities in this – that we can only say about them what we can extract by deductive means from what we have explicitly put into their defining characterization. These abstract entities do not have nongeneric properties since each is a "lowest species" unto itself.

We thus arrive at the next principal thesis of these deliberations:

Thesis 4: *The Transdenumerability of Facts.* The manifold of fact is transdenumerably infinite.

The idea of a complete listing of all facts is manifestly impracticable. Consider the following statement: "*The list F of stated facts fails to have this statement on it.*" But now suppose this statement is on the list. It clearly does not state a fact, so the list is after all not a list of the facts (contrary to hypothesis). And so it must be left off the list. But then that list will not be complete because the statement is true. Facts, that is to say, can never be listed *in toto* because there will always be further facts – facts about the entire list itself – that a supposedly complete list could not manage to register.

This conclusion can be rendered more graphic by the following considerations. Suppose that the list F

$$F: f_1, f_2, f_3, \cdots$$

were to constitute a *complete* enumeration of all facts. And now consider the statement

$$(Z) \text{ the list } F \text{ takes the form } f_1, f_2, f_3, \cdots$$

By hypothesis, this statement will present a fact. So if F is indeed a complete listing of *all* facts, then there will be an integer k such that

$$Z = f_k.$$

Accordingly, Z itself will occupy the k-th place on the F listing, so that

$$f_k = \text{the list } L \text{ takes the form } f_1, f_2, f_3, \cdots f_k, \cdots$$

But this would require f_k to be an expanded version of itself, which is absurd. With the k-th position of the F listing *already* occupied by f_k we cannot also squeeze that complex f_k-involving thesis into it.

The crux here is simply that any supposedly complete listing of facts

$$f_1, f_2, f_3 \cdots$$

will itself exhibit, as a whole, certain features that none of its individual members can encompass. Once those individual entries are fixed and the series is defined, there will be further facts about that series-as-a-whole that its members themselves cannot articulate.

Moreover, the point at issue can also be made via an analogue of the diagonal argument that is standardly used to show that no list of real numbers can manage to include all of them, thereby establishing the transdenumerability of the reals. Let us begin by imagining a supposedly complete inventory of *independent* facts, using logic to streamline the purported fact inventory into a condition of greater informative tidiness through the elimination of inferential redundancies, so that every remaining item adds some information to what has gone before. The argument for the transdenumerability of fact can now be developed as follows. Let us suppose (for the sake of *reductio ad absurdum* argumentation) that the inventory

$$f_1, f_2, f_3, \ldots$$

represents our (nonredundant but yet purportedly *complete*) listing of facts. Then by the supposition of *factuality* we have $(\forall i) f_i$. And further by the supposition of *completeness* we have it that

$$(\forall p)(p \rightarrow (\exists i)[f_i \rightarrow p]).$$

Moreover, by the aforementioned supposition of *non-redundancy*, each member of the sequence adds something quite new to what has gone before.

$$(\forall i)(\forall j)[i < j \rightarrow {\sim}[(f_1 \& f_2 \& \ldots \& f_i) \rightarrow f_j)].$$

Consider now the following course of reasoning.

(1) $(\forall i) f_i$ by "factuality"
(2) $(\forall j) f_j \rightarrow (\exists i)(f_i \rightarrow (\forall j) f_j)$ from (1) by "completeness" via the substitution of $(\forall j) f_j$ for p
(3) $(\exists i)(f_i \rightarrow (\forall j) f_j)$ from (1), (2)

But (3) contradicts non-redundancy. This *reductio ad absurdum* of our hypothesis indicates that facts are necessarily too numerous for complete enumeration.

More Facts Than Truths

In such circumstances, no purportedly comprehensive listing of truths can actually manage to encompass all facts. The long and short of it is that the domain of reality-characterizing fact inevitably transcends the limits of our capacity to *express* it, and *a fortiori* those of our capacity to canvass completely. The realm of fact is endlessly complex, detailed, and diversified in its makeup. And the limitedness of our recursively constituted linguistic resources thus means that our characterizations of the real will always fall short.[16] We arrive at

Thesis 5. *There are quantitatively more facts than truths* seeing that the facts are too numerous for enumerabilty.

The basic reason the domain of fact is ampler than that of truth is that language cannot capture the entirety of fact. It is not only possible but (apparently) likely that we live in a world that is not digital but analogue and whose manifold of states of affairs is simply too rich to be fully comprehended by our linguistically digital means. To all visible appearances the domain of fact transcends the limits of our capacity to *express* it, and *a fortiori* those of our capacity to canvass it. In confronting any landscape in nature, our representation of it in propositional discourse or thought – our description-scape, so to speak – is invariably far less complex than the real scene and inevitably suppresses a vast amount of detail. (Even the physics of discrete quanta requires continuous – and thus nondiscrete – parameters for its characterization.)

Truth is to fact what film is to reality – a merely discretized approximation. Cognition, being bound to language, is digital and sequentially linear. Reality, by contrast, is analogue and replete with feedback loops and nonsequentially systemic interrelations. It should thus not be seen as all that surprising that the two cannot be brought into smooth alignment. The comparative limitedness of truth that can

---

[16] Even in matters of actual linguistic practice we find an embarrassing shortcoming of words. The difficulty in adapting a compact vocabulary to the complexities of a diversified world are betokened by the pervasive phenomenon of polysemy – the contextualized pluralism of varied senses and differentiated uses of the same words in different semantic and grammatical categories. On this phenomenon see Hubert Cuyckens and Britta Zawada (eds.), *Polysemy in Cognitive Linguistics* (Amsterdam: John Benjamins, 2003).

be encapsulated in language points to an inevitable limitedness of knowledge.

Noninstantiable Properties and Vagrant Predicates

In this context of cognitive limits the cognitive intractability of certain temporalized issues has significant implications. Thus consider such questions as those already mentioned:

- What is an example of a problem that will never be considered by any human being?
- What is an example of an idea that will never occur to any human being?

There are sound reasons of general principle (the potential infinitude of problems and ideas; the inherent finitude of human intelligence) to hold that the items at issue in these questions do actually exist as problems that will never be considered or ideas that will never occur. But it seems altogether plausible that other (nonhuman) hypothetically envisionable intelligences could answer these questions correctly.

However, we can also contemplate the prospect of globally intractable questions – questions that, despite having correct answers, are nevertheless such that nobody (among finite intelligences at least) can possibly be in a position to answer them (in the strict sense described at the outset). With issues of absolutely unrestricted generality there will be many examples of this:

- an idea that has never occurred to anybody
- an occurrence that no one ever mentions
- a person who has passed into total oblivion
- a never-formulated question
- an idea no one any longer mentions

Yet while there undoubtedly are such items, they of course cannot possibly be instantiated. Accordingly, the corresponding example-demanding questions are inherently unanswerable insolubilia.

In all such cases, the particular items that would render a contention of the format $(\exists u)Fu$ true are *referentially inaccessible*: to indicate any of them individually and specifically as instantiations of the predicate at issue is *ipso facto* to unravel them as so-characterized items. And so, non-instantiability itself is certainly not something that is noninstantiable: many instances are available along the following lines:

- a never-stated contention (truth, theory, etc.)
- a never-mentioned topic (idea, object, etc.)
- a truth (a fact) no one has ever realized (learned, stated)
- someone whom everyone has forgotten
- a never-identified culprit
- an issue no one has thought about since the 16th century

In the light of these considerations, the positivist dogma that a question can qualify as empirically meaningful only if it is in principle possible for a finite knower to answer it (correctly) becomes problematic. Cognitive positivism is not a plausible prospect.

The conception of an applicable but nevertheless noninstantiable predicate comes to the fore at this point. Such predicates are "vagrant" in the sense of *having no known address or fixed abode*. Though they indeed have applications, these cannot be specifically instanced – they cannot be pinned down and located in a particular spot. Accordingly,

F is a *vagrant* predicate if $(\exists u) Fu$ is true while nevertheless Fu_0 is false for every specifically identified u_0.

For the sake of contrast, consider such further uninstitutable predicates as these:

- a book no one has ever read
- a sunset never witnessed by any member of homo sapiens

Such items may be difficult to instantiate – but certainly not impossible. The former could be instantiated by author and title; the latter by place and date. In neither case will an instantiation unravel that item as described. Being read is not indispensably essential to books, nor being seen to sunsets: being an unread book or being an unwitnessed sunset involves no contradiction in terms. By contrast, however, with actual vagrancy, epistemic inaccessibility is built into the specification at issue. Here we have predicates of such a sort that one can show on the basis of general principles that there must be items to which they apply, while nevertheless one can also establish that no such items can ever be concretely identified.[17]

The existence of vagrant predicates shows that applicability and instantiability do not amount to the same thing. By definition, vagrant predicates will be applicable: there indeed are items to which they apply. However, this circumstance will always have to be something that must be claimed on the basis of general principles; doing so by means of concretely identified instances is, by hypothesis, infeasible.

While vagrant predicates are by nature noninstantiable, we can nevertheless use them to *individuate* items that we can never *identify*. For instance, with regard to "the youngest unknown (i.e., never-to-be-identified) victim of the eruption of Krakatoa," one can make various true claims about the so-individuated person – for example that he or she was alive at the time of Krakatoa's eruption. One can certainly *discuss* that individual as such – that is, as an individual – even though, by hypothesis, we cannot manage to *identify* him or her. Predicative vagrancy thus reinforces the distinction between mere individuation and actual identification.

If *F* is a variant predicate, then *Fix* has no true substitution instances: *Fa* is in fact false for every specifiable value of *a*. But nevertheless $(\exists x)Fx$ is going to be true. (The logic of vagrant predicates is emphatically not "intuitionistic," and the substitutional interpretation of the quantifiers is certainly not going to work.)

It will not have escaped the acute reader that all of the demonstrably unanswerable questions and unknowable facts at issue in the present discussion relate to issues of cognition and knowledge themselves. Clearly if this is the best that can be done in this direction an interesting conclusion follows – namely, that unknowability automatically arises with the emergence of knowers. In a universe without them there could possibly be a total absence of in-principle unknowable facts. But once finitely intelligent beings emerge in the world, unanswerable questions and unknowable facts emerge inexorably in their wake. All of those vagrant predicates involve some limitation of knowledge. For

---

[17] Reference, to be sure, does not require identification. A uniquely characterizing description on the order of "the tallest person in the room" will single out a particular individual without specifically identifying him.

an omniscient God, the phenomenon of vagrancy vanishes. But we, of course, cannot claim to be in this position.

Musical Chairs Once More

It is instructive at this point to consider once more the analogy of Musical Chairs. Of course, any individual player *can/might* be seated. And the same goes for any team or group with one exception: *the whole lot*. But since the manifold of knowable truth is denumerable and the manifold of fact in toto is not, then (as in our Musical Chairs example) the range of the practicable will not, cannot encompass the whole. (And note then while a team of individuals is not an individual, a complex of facts will nevertheless constitute a fact.)

With regard to language too we once again confront a Musical Chairs situation. Conceivably, language-at-large might, in the abstract, manage to encompass nondenumerably many instances – particularly so if we indulge the prospect of idealization and resort to Bolzano's *Saetze an sich*, Frege's *denkerlose Gedanken*, and the like. But given the granular structure of a universe pervaded by atoms and molecules, only a denumerable number of language-using creatures can ever be squeezed into the fabric of the cosmos. And so the realistically practicable possibilities of *available* languages are at best denumerable.

When reality and language play their game of Musical Chairs, some facts are bound to be left in the lurch when the music of language stops. The discrepancy manifests itself in the difference between *any* and *every*. Any candidate can possibly be accommodated. (We have $(\forall x) \Diamond (\exists y) Syx$.) But it is not possible to accommodate every candidate. (We do *not* have $\Diamond (\forall x) (\exists y) Syx$.) The limits of knowledge are thus in the final analysis quantitative. The crux of the problem is a discrepancy of numbers. They root in the Musical Chairs Perplex – in the fact that the realm of fact is too vast for the restrictive confines of propositionalized language.

And this situation has important cognitive ramifications that are brought to view by the following line of thought:

1. Everything there is – (and indeed even presumably everything there possibly can be) – has an idiosyncratic property, some

feature, no doubt complex and perhaps composite, that holds for it and it alone. (Metaphysical principle)

2. The possession of such a unique characteristic property cannot obtain in virtue of the fact that the item at issue is of a certain natural kind or generic type. It can only obtain in virtue of something appertaining to this item individually and specifically.

3. Accordingly, for anything whatsoever, there is a fact – that that thing has that particular idiosyncratic property – that you can know only if you can individuate and specify that particular thing.

4. The inherent limitations of language mean that there are more things that it is possible to individuate and specify.

The inevitability of unknown facts emerges at once from these considerations of general principle.

The reality is that the domain of fact is ampler than the domain of truth so that language cannot capture the entirety of fact. We live in a world that is not digital but analogue and so the manifold of its states of affairs is simply too rich to be fully comprehended by our linguistically digital means.[18] The domain of fact inevitably transcends the limits of our capacity to *express* it, and *a fortiori* those of our capacity to canvass it in overt detail. Truth is to fact what moving pictures are to reality – a merely discretized approximation.

To be sure, the numerical discrepancy at issue with the Musical Chairs Perplex does no more than establish the existence of *unknown* facts. It does not got so far as to establish the existence of facts that are *unknowable*, facts that cannot, as a matter of principle, possibly be known. To see what can be done in this line we shall have to look at matters in a different light.

There clearly is, however, one fact that is unstatable to language and thereby unknowable by creatures whose knowledge is confined to the linguistically formulatable. This is the grand mega-fact consisting

---

[18] Wittgenstein writes "logic is not a body of doctrine, but a mirror-image of the world" (*Tractatus*, 6.13). This surely gets it wrong: logic is one instrumentality (among others) for organizing our thought about the world, and this thought is (at best and at most) a venture in *describing* or *conceiving* the world and its modus operandi in a way that – life being what it is – will inevitably be imperfect, and incomplete. And so any talk of mirroring is a totally unrealistic exaggeration here.

of the amalgamation of all facts whatever. For language-dependent knowers can at most and at best have cognitive access to a denumerable number of facts, whereas factuality itself in principle encompasses a nondenumerable quantity.

And a very important point is at issue here. With Musical Chairs we know that someone will be unseated, but we cannot (given the ordinary contingencies) manage to say *who* this will be. And with facts, which from a cognitive point of view reduplicate the Musical Chairs situation, we also cannot manage to say which facts will be unknown. For here too there is a lot of room for contingency. But there is one very big difference. With Musical Chairs the totality of individuals, while of course not reliable, does not combine to form a single unseatable mega-individual. But the totality of facts – which cannot possibly be known – does indeed combine to form one grand unknowable megafact.

So here indeed we have managed to individuate a particular unknowable fact, namely, the all-encompassing megafact. But of course while we know *that* it is unknowable, we do not know *what* it is. We have *individuated* but not *identified* it. So here, as elsewhere, the details of our ignorance are hidden from our sight.

Just what does this mean in the larger scheme of things?

Coda: Against Cognitive Nominalism

If we are going to be realistic about it – in both the ordinary and the philosophical sense of this term – then we still have to resist the temptation of a nominalistic textualism that identifies the nature of reality with what we can manage to know about it. However, we are also well advised to avoid succumbing to the siren call of mysticism. Certainly the present deliberations regarding unknowable fact do not lead to this destination. Granted, given the limitations of language, there will of course be things that have to go unsaid – facts with respect to what words literally fail us. But there is no reason to join with Wittgenstein in characterizing this as "the mystical" (*Tractatus*, 6.522). These considerations afford no automatic reason for thinking that what is unsaid is going to be significantly different *in kind* from the things one can say, no constraining reason to see them as somehow strange and different – any more than those individuals who go unseated in Musical

Chairs need be strange and different. What makes for the unsayability of these things is not their inherent ineffability but merely that there just are too many of them. No doubt reality is stranger than we think. But the ground of *this* circumstance will ultimately lie in the nature of reality and not in the limitedness of language.

Appendix: Further Implications

It is worthwhile to note that the numerical discrepancy between truths and facts that textuality imposes recurs time and again in other contexts, and in particular between these:

- names and entities
- statements and possibilities
- descriptions and objects
- novels and plots
- instructions and actions
- explanations and phenomena

The same disproportion between the verbal and the ontological realm occurs throughout. While in each case the former is a verbalized placeholder for the latter, there just are not enough of the former to go around.

In particular, consider names. Of course everything is capable of being named. Nothing is name resistant. We could (as someone has quipped) simply name everything Charlie. The real question is whether everything could have a unique name characteristic of itself alone: an identifying name.

Now everything that has actually been identified could be named via the specification: "the item identified in such and such a way." Or at least this would work if the identification process answered to some verbalized formula. But even supposing this to be the case, the question remains: Are there enough verbal/textual identifiers to go around? Can everything that has an identity be individuated by verbalized formulas?

And the answer is categorically negative. Select any language you please – take your pick. As long as it – like any other human language – is produced recursively it will only have countably many expressions (words, sentences, texts). But we know full well that the number of objects is transdenumerable: uncountably infinite. (Think of the real numbers, for example.) So there just are not enough names to encompass everything. In musical chairs not everybody gets to be seated. In reality not everything gets to be named.

Of course, things will stand differently if we radically revise the concept of *language*. Thus if we are prepared to countenance a thing language (rather than a word language) we could adopt the rule that everything names itself. And then of course everything is at once namable and named. But this sort of thing is clearly cheating.

And so while nothing is textually name-resistant and everything is namable in the sense of being able, in principle, to bear a verbal name, the possibility of realizing this prospect across the board – with everything whatsoever actually bearing a name – is precluded by the general principles of the situation.[19]

[19] This Appendix has benefited from exchanges with C. Anthony Anderson.

8

On the Limits of Knowledge

A Kantian Perspective on Cognitive Finitude

(1) It is in principle impossible ever to give an example of an unknowable fact. (2) While universalizations do enable us to assert truths about nonsurveyable totalities, such totalities nevertheless serve to demarcate us as cognitively finite beings. (3) For general facts regarding an open-ended group will – when contingent and not law-inherent – open the door to facts that are beyond the cognitive grasp of finite knowledge. (4) Nevertheless, as Kant insightfully saw it, the realm of knowledge – of ascertainable fact – while indeed limited, is nevertheless unbounded.

Limits of Knowledge

The cognitive beings that will concern us here are language-dependent finite intelligences. These by their very nature are bound to be imperfect knowers. For the factual information at their disposal by way of propositional knowledge that something or other is the case will – unlike practical how-to knowledge – have to be verbally formulated. And language-encompassed textuality is – as we have seen – outdistanced by the facts themselves. Just what is one to make of the numerical disparity between facts and truths, between what is knowable in theory and what our finite intelligences can actually manage to know? Just what does this disproportion portend?

It means that our knowledge of fact is incomplete – and inevitably so! – because we finite intelligences lack the means for reality's comprehensive characterization. Reality in all its blooming buzzing complexity is too rich for faithful representation by the recursive and enumerable resources of our language. We do and must recognize the limitations of our cognition, acknowledging that we cannot justifiably equate facticity with what can explicitly be known by us through the resources of language. And what transpires here for the circumstantial situation of us humans obtains equally for any other sort of finite intelligence as well. Any physically realizable sort of cognizing being can articulate – and thus can know – only a part or aspect of the real.

The situation as regards knowing facts is akin to that of counting integers – specifically in the following regards:[1]

1. The manifold of integers is inexhaustible. We can never come to grips with all of them as particular individuals. Nevertheless –
2. Further progress is always possible: in principle we can always go beyond whatever point we have so far managed to reach. Nevertheless –
3. Further progress gets ever more cumbersome. In moving onward we must be always more prolix and make use of increasingly elaborate symbol complexes so that greater demands in time, effort, and resources are unavoidable. Accordingly –
4. In actual practice there will be only so much that we can effectively manage to do. The possibilities that obtain in principle can never be fully realized in practice. However –
5. Such limitations nowise hamper the prospects of establishing various correct generalizations about the manifold of integers in its abstract entirety.

And a parallel situation characterizes the cognitive condition of all finite intelligences whose cognitive operations have to proceed by a symbolic process that functions by language. Inductive inquiry, like counting, never achieves completeness. There is always more to be done, and in both cases we can always do better by doing more. But it also means that much will always remain undone – that we can never do it all.

But are those unknown facts actually unknowable? The answer is neither yes nor no. As already foreshadowed above, it all depends on exactly how one construes the possibilistic matter of "knowability."

---

[1] We here take "counting" to be a matter of indicating integers by name – for example, as "thirteen" or "13" – rather than descriptively, as per "the first prime after eleven."

Using *Kxf* to abbreviate "the individual x knows the fact f," there will clearly be two rather different ways in which the existence of an inherently unknowable fact can be claimed, namely "Some fact is necessarily unknown."

$$(\exists f)\,\Box\,(\forall x)\sim Kxf \text{ or equivalently} \sim(\forall f)\Diamond(\exists x)\,Kxf$$

and "Necessarily, some fact is unknown"

$$\Box\,(\exists f)\,(\forall x)\sim Kxf \text{ or equivalently} \sim\Diamond(\forall f)\,(\exists x)\,Kxf.$$

The difference in the quantifier placement in the preceding two formulas is crucial when one contemplates the idea that all facts are knowable. Now the first of these two contentions logically entails the second. And this second is in the circumstances inevitable, there being more facts than finite humans ever will or can know. However, the first, stronger contention is clearly false. For as long as the nonexistence of an omniscient God is not a *necessary* circumstance there can be no fact that is of necessity unknown.

But of course even though there are – or may well be – *unknowable facts* (in the indicated sense of this term so that for some fact f we have $\Box\,(\forall x)\sim Kxf$), such a fact can never be identified as such, namely *as a fact*, since doing so is effectively to claim knowledge of it. It is thus in principle impossible for us ever to give an example of one of the unidentifiable facts even though there must be some. And nothing more strikingly betokens the imperfection and limitedness of our knowledge than the ironic circumstance of the uneliminable incompleteness of our knowledge regarding our knowledge itself, which arises because we do not – and cannot – know the details of our own ignorance (i.e., cannot possibly know what it is that we do not know).[2]

Cognitive Finitude

First the good news. Generalizations can of course refer to *everything*. Bishop Butler's "Everything is what it is and not another thing" holds with unrestricted universality. And once continuous quantities

[2] This discussion has profited from the constructive comments of several Pittsburgh colleagues, including Jason Dickinson, Mickey Perloff, and Laura Ruetsche.

are introduced, the range of *inferentially available* statements becomes uncountable. "The length of the table exceeds *x* inches." Once known, this straightaway opens the door to uncountably knowable consequences. And fortunately, a case-by-case determination is not generally needed to validate generalizations. We can establish claims about groups larger than we can ever hope to inventory. Recourse to arbitrary instances, the process of indirect proof by *reductio ad absurdum*, and induction (mathematical and scientific) all afford procedures for achieving generality knowledge beyond the reach of an exhaustive case-by-case check.

But will this *always* be so? Or are there also general truths whose determination would require the exhaustive surveying of all specific instances of a totality too large for our range of vision?

At this point our cognitive finitude becomes a crucial consideration and the difference between finite and infinite knowers becomes of fundamental importance and requires closer elucidation. For an "infinite knower" need not and should not be construed as an *omniscient* knower – one from whom nothing knowable is concealed (and so who knows, for example, who will be elected U.S. president in the year 2200). Rather, what is at issue is a knower who can manage to know in individualized detail an infinite number of independent facts. (Such a knower might, for example, be able to answer such a question as, "Will the decimal expansion of π always continue to agree at some future point with that of $\sqrt{2}$ for 100 decimal places?") Finite knowers cannot manage this sort of thing.

Finite knowers can, of course, know universal truths. After all, we must acknowledge the prospect of inductive knowledge of general laws; we will have it that a knower can unproblematically know – for example – that "All dogs eat meat."[3] But what finite knowers *cannot* manage is to know this sort of thing *in detail* rather than at the level of generality. They cannot know specifically of every *u* in that potentially infinite range that *Fu* obtains – that is, while they can know collectively *that all individuals have F*, they cannot know distributively

---

3 To be sure, the prospect of inductively secured knowledge of laws is a philosophically controversial issue. But this is not the place to pursue it. (For the author's position see his *Induction* (Oxford: Blackwell, 1980).)

of every individual that it has F – something they could not do without knowing who they individually are.

So the issue now before us is that of the question of general truths that can be known *only* by assessing the situation of an untractable manifold of individual cases.

Surd Facts and Unknowability

One cannot, of course, provide concrete examples of facts that are unknowable to finite knowers, seeing that a claim to factuality automatically carries a claim to knowledge in its wake. However while we cannot know specifically *what* is such a fact, we can certainly substantiate the claim generally *that* there are such things. Let us consider this situation more closely.

Given any collection of items there are two importantly different kinds of general properties: those that all members of the collection DO have in common, and those that all members of the collection MUST have in common. The latter are the *necessitated* general features of the collection, the former its *contingently geared* features. Thus that all prime numbers greater than 2 are odd is a necessity-geared feature of this set of primes. Or consider the set of all U.S. presidents. That all of them are native born and that all of them are over 35 years of age is a necessitated general feature of the collection in view of our Constitution's stipulations. However, that all were born outside Hawaii will (if indeed true) be a contingently geared feature of the collection that is nowise necessitated by the general principles of the Constitution.

Now the crucial consideration for present purposes is that while the *necessary* features of a collection must inhere in (and be derivable from) the generalities that govern the collection at issue as a matter of principle, its *contingent* features will be *surd* in that they cannot be established on the basis of general principles.

Accordingly, a general fact $F(C)$ regarding a collection C is surd if whenever a set of premises entails this fact, then every item belonging to C must secure specific individual mention in one or another of these premises. We thus have it that $F(C)$ represents a surd fact about C if

Whenever $P_1, P_2, \ldots P_n \vdash F(C)$ then every member of C must receive specific mention in one or another of Pi.

And of course since $F(C) \vdash F(C)$ this means that $F(C)$ must itself be so constructed as to involve a specific mention of all C-members. The salient point, at any rate, is that such a feature can only be ascribed to a collection on the basis of a comprehensive one-by-one examination of its members.

For the sake of an example, let the object under consideration be the material numbers (1, 2, 3, etc.) and make the set

$$S = \{1, 3, 17\}.$$

The feature of S represented by "All S-members are either odd or even" is a non-surd feature of this set. (Given that integers are at issue, we need not inspect its members to assure ourselves that this generalization obtains): that "all" can be construed collectively. But the feature of S represented by "All S-members are < 20" is indeed a surd feature of this set. Its characterizing S is a fact that cannot be assured without inspecting each one of its members. Here, that "all" must be construed distributively.

So when and if contingent generalities actually hold for a collection, this can be ascertained only through a case-by-case check of its entire membership. And this means that *finite knowers can never decisively establish a surd/contingent general feature of an infinite collection.* For whenever a generality holds for a collection on a merely contingent basis, this is something that we finite intelligences can never determine with categorical assurance because determination of *such* kind-pervasively surd would thus require an item-by-item check, which is by hypothesis impracticable for us.

It must also be presumed to be a fact that as long as the paper exists, every issue of the *New York Times* will be such that the word THE occurs more than five times on its front page. This is almost certainly a fact. But since this assertion cannot be settled by general principles (laws) but requires a case-by-case check it is generally characterized as *surd*. And such a property of something is contingent: it cannot be accounted for on the basis of the general principles at issue.

Consider now a set of objects of a certain sort *S* that is infinite or interminably open-ended (lions, say, or sunrises at Acapulco). And let *P* be a surd/contingent property of some *S*-item *X* which, while in principle is applicable to *S*-members, is nevertheless unique to *X*– that is, is such that no other *S*-member actually has *P*. Note that now this uniqueness could only be determined on a case-by-case check across the whole range of *S*. Accordingly, that *X* is unique within *S* in point of *P*-possession is (by hypothesis) a truth that no finite intelligence could ascertain, seeing that an item-by-item canvass of an infinite/indefinite range is beyond its capacity. Such claims illustrate the prospect of truths beyond the cognitive grasp of finite knowers.

Of course, "unknowably true" is a *vagrant* predicate in the sense of the proceeding chapter – one that has no determinate address in that it admits of no identifiable instance. Instantiating this sort of thing can be done only at the level of schematic generality and not that of concrete instantiation. For while we can convince ourselves – for good reason – that there indeed are such things, it nevertheless remains in principle impracticable to provide examples of them.

Larger Lessons: Isaiah's Law

Something about which we cannot possibly be mistaken is our belief that we are beings who make mistakes. And analogously, one regard in which our knowledge cannot be incomplete – something that it is effectively impossible for us to overlook – is the fact of our cognitive finitude itself, the realization that we do not actually "know it all."

However, the situation regarding our cognitive limits is not quite as bleak as it may seem. For even though the thought and knowledge of finite beings is destined to be ever incomplete, it nevertheless has no fixed and determinate limits. Return to our analogy. As to our counting integers, there is a limit beyond which we never *will* get. But there is no limit beyond which we never *can* get.

The line of thought operative in these deliberations was already mooted by Kant:

[I]n natural philosophy, human reason admits of *limits* ("excluding limits," *Schranken*) but not of *boundaries* ("terminating limits," *Grenzen*), namely, it admits that something indeed lies without it, at which it can never arrive, but not that it will at any point find completion in its internal progress. . . . [T]he possibility of new discoveries is infinite: and the same is the case with the discovery of new properties of nature, of new powers and laws by continued experience and its rational combination.[4]

Given the inevitable discrepancy – and numerical disproportion – between our propositionally encodable information about the real and the factual complexity of reality itself, we have to be cautious regarding the kind of scientific realism we endorse. Any claims that reality in its details is exactly as the science of the day claims it to be is (irrespective of how the calendar reads) extremely questionable. This is something that already became apparent early in the discussion of the security/definiteness trade-off. And everything that the subsequent discussion has brought to light only serves to substantiate this conclusion in greater detail.

Some writers analogize the cognitive exploration of the realm of fact to the geographic exploration of the earth. But this analogy is profoundly misleading. For the earth has a finite and measurable surface, and so even when some part of it is unexplored *terra incognita* its magnitude and limits can be assessed in advance. Nothing of the kind obtains in the cognitive domain. The ratio and relationship of known truth to knowable fact is subject to no fixed and determinable proportion. Geographic exploration can expect eventual completeness; cognitive exploration cannot.

All the same, there can be no doubt that ignorance exacts its price in incomprehension. And here it helps to consider the matter in a somewhat theological light. The world we live in is a manifold that is not of our making but of Reality's – of God's, if you will.

---

4 *Prolegomena to any Future Metaphysics*, sect. 57. Compare the following passage from Charles Sanders Peirce: "For my part, I cannot admit the proposition of Kant – that there are certain impassable bounds to human knowledge. . . . The history of science affords illustrations enough of the folly of saying that this, that, or the other can never be found out. Auguste Comte said that it was clearly impossible for man ever to learn anything of the chemical constitution of the fixed stars, but before his book had reached its readers the discovery which he had announced as impossible had been made. Legendre said of a certain proposition in the theory of numbers that, while it appeared to be true, it was most likely beyond the powers of the human mind to prove it; yet the next writer on the subject gave six independent demonstrations of the theorem." (*Collected Papers* [Cambridge, MA: Harvard University Press, 1931–58], 2nd ed., vol. VI, sect. 6.556.)

What is at issue might be called Isaiah's Law on the basis of the verse: "For as the heavens are higher than the earth, so are my ways higher than your ways, and my thoughts than your thoughts."[5] A fundamental law of epistemology is at work here – to wit, that *a mind of lesser power is for this very reason unable to understand adequately the workings of a mind of greater power*. To be sure, the weaker mind can doubtless realize *that* the stronger can solve problems that the lesser cannot. But it cannot understand *how* it is able to do so. An intellect that can only just manage to do well at tic-tac-toe cannot possibly comprehend the ways of one that is expert at chess.

Consider in this light the vast disparity of computational power between a mathematical tyro like most of us and a mathematical prodigy like Ramanujan. Not only cannot our tyro manage to answer the number-theoretic question that such a genius resolves in the blink of an eye, but the tyro cannot even begin to understand the processes and procedures that the Indian genius employs. As far as the tyro is concerned, it is all sheer wizardry. No doubt once an answer is given he can check its correctness. But actually finding the answer is something that lesser intellect cannot manage – the how of the business lies beyond its grasp. And for much the same sort of reason, a mind of lesser power cannot discover what the question-resolving limits of a mind of greater power are. It can never say with warranted assurance where the limits of question-resolving power lie. (In some instances it may be able to say what's in and what's out, but never map the dividing boundary.)

It is not simply that a more powerful mind will know more facts than a less powerful one, but that its conceptual machinery is ampler in encompassing ideas and issues that lie altogether outside the conceptual horizon of its less powerful compeers.

Now insofar as the relation of a lesser toward a higher intelligence is substantially analogous to the relation between an earlier state of science and a later state, some instructive lessons emerge. It is not that Aristotle could not have comprehended quantum theory; he was a very smart fellow and could certainly have learned. But what he could not have done was to formulate quantum theory within his own conceptual framework, his own familiar terms of reference. The very

[5] *Isaiah*, 58:9.

ideas at issue lay outside the conceptual horizon of Aristotle's science, and like present-day students he would have had to master them from the ground up. Just this sort of thing is at issue with the relation of a less powerful intelligence to a more powerful one. It has been said insightfully that from the vantage point of a less developed technology, another substantially advanced technology is indistinguishable from magic. And exactly the same holds for a more advanced *conceptual* (rather than physical) technology.

It is instructive to contemplate in this light the hopeless difficulties encountered nowadays in the popularization of physics – of trying to characterize the implications of quantum theory and relativity theory for cosmology into the subscientific language of everyday life. A classic *obiter dictum* of Niels Bohr is relevant: "We must be clear that, when it comes to atoms, language can be used only as in poetry." Alas, we have to recognize that in philosophy, too, we are in something of the same position. In the history of culture, Homo sapiens began his quest for knowledge in the realm of poetry. And in the end it seems that we are destined to remain at this starting point in some respects.

All the same, our cognitive limitedness as finite beings notwithstanding, there nevertheless are no boundaries – no *determinate* limits – to the manifold of discoverable fact. And here Kant was right – even on the Leibnizian principles considered earlier in the discussion. For while the cognitive range of finite beings is indeed limited, it is also boundless because it is not limited in a way that blocks the prospect of cognitive access to ever new and ongoingly more informative facts that afford us an ever ampler and ever more adequate account of reality.

Conclusion

In concluding, a brief survey of the principal theses may be in order. They stand as follows:

Duhem's Law of Security/Detail Complimentarity. The security and detail of our knowledge stand in a relation of inverse proportionality. (Chapter 1)

Kant's Principle of Cognitive Systematization. Knowledge, in the qualitative and honorific sense of the term, is a matter of the extent to which information is coherently systematized. (Chapter 2)

Spencer's Law of Cognitive Development. Cognitive progress is accompanied by complexification and can be assessed in terms of the taxonomic complexity of the information manifold at hand. However, this complexity is not proportional of the *amount* of information, but to its *logarithm*. And this yields –

Kant's Principle of Question Propagation. The progress of knowledge-development in the course of resolving our questions always brings new questions to light. (Chapter 4)

Gibbon's Law of Logarithmic Returns. The quantity of knowledge interest in a body of information is proportional not to the size of this body, but merely to the logarithm thereof. (Chapter 4)

Adams's Thesis of Exponential Growth. Throughout recent history the body of scientific information has been growing exponentially. But, in view of Gibbon's Law, this means that cognitive progress in terms of actual knowledge has been growing at a rate that is merely linear and thereby stable. (Chapter 5)

Quality/Quantity Alignment. The lower levels of informative quality information that define the lesser degrees of "knowledge" are in volumetric alignment with the λ-power ($0 < \lambda \leq 1$) of the total amount of information at hand. (Chapter 6)

Zipf's Law. With objects rank-ordered by measurable size, the product of this size with the number of objects of at least that size is constant. And with cognitive importance as size this puts quality and quantity into a relationship of complementarity. (Chapter 6)

Quality Retardation. Cognitive progress at lesser levels of what is not so much knowledge as high-quality information proceeds at a pace that is ever slower as the bar of quality is raised. (Chapter 6)

Leibniz's Thesis of Cognitive Limitation. Mere volumetric considerations indicate that knowledge cannot keep up with fact. Seeing that our knowledge is language-bound, it is inherently unable to accommodate reality's unending complexity of details. (Chapter 7)

Isaiah's Law. A mind of a lesser power cannot fathom the workings of one of greater power: some of its operations are bound to appear as "magic." (Chapter 8)

Kant's Perspective on Cognitive Finitude. While the realm of knowledge – of *ascertainable* fact – is indeed limited, it is nevertheless unbounded. (Chapter 8)

Taken together these various theses and ideas provide a quantitative perspective on knowledge and its limits. They thus combine to clarify the situation that confronts a finite intelligence in its effort to gain a cognitive grip on an endlessly complex and in some respects unavoidably inscrutable world.

Bibliography

Adams, Henry, *The Education of Henry Adams* (Boston, 1918; privately printed already in 1907).

Amaldi, Edoardo, "The Unity of Physics," *Physics Today*, 261 (September, 1973), pp. 23–29.

Auger, Pierre, *Current Trends in Scientific Research* (Paris, 1961; UNESCO Publications), pp. 15–16.

Basalla, G., William Coleman, and R. H. Kargon [eds.], *Victorian Science: A Self-Portrait through the Presidential Addresses of the British Association for the Advancement of Science* (New York: New York Academy of Sciences, 1970).

Beeley, Philip, "Leibniz on the Limits of Human Knowledge," *Leibniz Review*, 13 (December 2003), pp. 93–97.

Borges, Jorge Luis, "The Library of Babel."

Brandon, Robert N., *Adaptation and Environment* (Princeton: Princeton University Press, 1990).

Cardwell, D. S. C., "The Professional Society" in Norman Kaplan (ed.), *Science and Society* (Chicago, 1965), pp. 86–91.

Cicero, *De natura deorum.*

Couturat, Louis, *La logique de Leibniz* (Paris: Alcan, 1901).

Cuyckens, Hubert, and Britta Zawada (eds.), *Polysemy in Cognitive Linguistics* (Amsterdam: John Benjamins, 2003).

David, Paul A., "Positive Feedback and Research Productivity in Science," in O. Granstrand (ed.), *The Economics of Technology* (Amsterdam: Elsevier, 1994), pp. 65–89.

Dolby, R. G. A., "Classification of the Sciences: The Nineteenth-Century Tradition" (unpublished study issued for its author by the University of Kent at Canterbury ca. 1975).

Doyle, A. Conan, *The Great Keinplatz Experiment* (1894).

Duhem, *La théorie physique: son objet, et sa structure* (Paris: Chevalier and Rivière, 1906); tr. by Philip P. Wiener, *The Aim and Structure of Physical Theory* (Princeton: Princeton University Press, 1954).

Dupré, John, *The Disorder of Things: Metaphysical Foundations of the Disunity of Science* (Cambridge, MA: Harvard University Press, 1993).

Eddington, Sir Arthur, *The Nature of the Physical World* (London: Macmillan, 1929), pp. 72–73.

Euclid, *Elements*.

Flint, Robert, *Philosophy as Scientia Scientiarun: A History of Classifications of the Sciences* (Edinburgh: W. Blackwood and Sons, 1904).

George, William, *The Scientist in Action* (London: Williams & Norgate, 1938).

Gibbon, Edward, *Memoirs of My Life* (Harmondworth, 1984).

Glass, Bentley, "Milestones and Rates of Growth in the Development of Biology," *Quarterly Review of Biology*, 54 (March 1979), pp. 31–53.

Goffin William, and Kenneth S. Warren, *Scientific Information Systems and the Principle of Solidarity* (New York: Praeger, 1981).

Gore, George, *The Art of Scientific Discovery* (London: Longmans, Green, 1878).

Heath, T. C., *The Works of Archimedes* (Cambridge: Cambridge University Press, 1897).

Holland, John H., *Hidden Order: How Adaptation Builds Complexity* (Reading, MA: Addison Wesley, 1995).

Holub, H. W., Gottfried Tappeiner, and Veronica Eberharter, "The Iron Law of Important Articles," *Southern Economic Journal*, 58 (1991), pp. 317–28.

Hugly, Philip, and Charles Sayward, "Can a Language Have Indenumerably Many Expressions?" *History and Philosophy of Logic*, 4, 1983.

International Survey of Book Production during the Last Decades (Paris: UNESCO, 1985).

Isaiah, 58:9.

Jevons, W. S., *The Principles of Science*, 2nd ed. (London: MacMillan, 1876).

Kant, Immanuel, *Critique of Pure Reason*.

Kant, Immanuel, *Prolegomena to any Future Metaphysics*.

Kaufmann, Stuart, *At Home in the Universe: To Search for the Laws of Self-Organization and Complexity* (New York: Oxford University Press, 1995).

Kuhn, Thomas S., *The Structure of Scientific Revolutions* (Chicago: University of Chicago Press, 1962).

Laudan, Larry, *Progress and Its Problems* (Berkeley: University of California Press, 1971).

Leibniz, G. W., *De l'horizon de la doctrine humaine*, ed. by Michael Fichant (Paris: Vrin, 1991).

Machlup, Fritz, *The Production and Distribution of Knowledge in the United States* (Princeton: Princeton University Press, 1962).

Mariétan Joseph, *Probléme de la classification des sciences d'Aristote à St. Thomas* (St. Maurice and Paris: Fribourg, 1901).

Mees, C. E. K., *The Path of Science* (New York: Wiley, 1946).

Newton, *Principia*.

Parat, M. V., *The Information Economy: Definition and Measurement* (Washington, DC: U.S. Department of Commerce, May 1977; OT Special Publication 77–12).

Peirce, Charles Sanders, *Collected Papers*, 8 vols. (Cambridge, MA: Harvard University Press, 1931–58).

Pelzholdt, Julius, *Bibliotheca Bibliographica* (Leipzig: W. Engelmann, 1866).

Petley, B. W., *The Fundamental Physical Constants and the Frontiers of Measurement* (Bristol: Hilger, 1985).

Planck, Max, *Vorträge und Erinnerungen*, 5th ed. (Stuttgart: Hirzel, 1949).

Price, Derek J., *Little Science, Big Science* (New York: Columbia University Press, 1963).

Price, Derek J., *Science since Babylon*, 2nd ed. (New Haven, CT: Yale University Press, 1975).

Price, Derek J., *Characteristics of Doctrinal Scientists and Engineers in the University System*, 1991 (Arlington, VA.: National Science Foundation, 1994); Document No. 94–307.

Rescher, Nicholas, *Dialectics* (Albany: State University of New York Press, 1977).

Rescher, Nicholas, *Scientific Progress* (Oxford: Blackwell, 1978).

Rescher, Nicholas, *Cognitive Systematization* (Oxford: Basil Blackwell, 1979).

Rescher, Nicholas, *Induction* (Oxford: Blackwell, 1980).

Rescher, Nicholas, "Leibniz and the Concept of a System" in his *Leibniz's Philosophy of Nature* (Dordrecht: D. Reidel, 1981), pp. 29–41.

Rescher, Nicholas, *The Limits of Science* (Berkeley and Los Angeles: University of California Press, 1984).

Rescher, Nicholas, *The Strife of Systems* (Pittsburgh: University of Pittsburgh Press, 1985).

Rescher, Nicholas, *Scientific Realism* (Dordrecht: D. Reidel, 1987).

Richardson, Ernest Cushing, *Classification: Theoretical and Practical*, 3rd. ed. (New York: H. W. Wilson, 1930).

Richtmyer, F. K., "The Romance of the Next Decimal Place," *Science*, 75 (1932), pp. 1–5.

Rousseau, J. J., *Contrat Social.*

Samuels, Ernest, *Henry Adams: The Major Phase* (Cambridge, MA, 1964).

Shields, Charles W., *Philosophia Ultima*, vol. II, *The History of the Sciences and the Logic of the Sciences or the Science of the Sciences* (New York: Scribner's 1888–1905), 3 vols.

Shockley, William, "On the Statistics of Productivity in Research," *Proceedings of the Institute of Radio Engineeers*, 45 (1957), pp. 279–90.

Spencer, Herbert, *First Principles*, 7th ed. (London: Appleton's, 1889); see sects. 14–17 of Part II, "The Law of Evolution." *Statistics of Science and Technology* (London: HMSO, 1970).

Strawson, P. F., "Truth," *Proceedings of the Aristotelian Society*, Supplementary Vol. 24, 1950, pp. 129–56.

Ulam, Stanislaw M., *Adventures of a Mathematician* (New York: Scribner's 1976).

Vollmer, H. M, and D. L. Mills, eds., *Professionalization* (Englewood Cliffs, NJ: Prentice Hall, 1966).

Wagner-Döbler, Roland, "Rescher's Principle of Decreasing Marginal Returns for Scientific Research," *Scientometrics*, 50 (2001), pp. 419–36.

Weinberg, Alvin M., "The Impact of Large-Scale Science on the United States," *Science,* 134 (1961; 21 July issue), pp. 161–64.

Weinberg, Steven, *Dreams of a Final Theory* (New York: Pantheon Books, 1992).

Weizsäcker, C. F. von., "The Unity of Physics" in Ted Bastin (ed.), *Quantum Theory and Beyond* (Cambridge: Cambridge University Press, 1971).

Wertheimer, F. H. et al., *Chemistry: Opportunities and Needs* (Washington, DC: National Academy of Sciences/National Research Council, 1965).

Wible, James R., "Rescher's Economic Philosophy of Science," *Journal of Economic Methodology,* vol. 1 (1994), pp. 314–29.

Wible, James R., *The Economic of Science* (London & New York: Routledge, 1998).

Wittgenstein, Ludwig, *Tractatus.*

Zipf, George K., *Human Behaviour and the Principle of Least Effort* (Boston: Addison-Wesley, 1949).

Index of Names

Adams, Henry, 45–55, 47n4, 107, 109
Amaldi, Edoardo, 25n15, 110
Anderson, C. Anthony, 94n19
Aquinas, St. Thomas, 13n2, 20
Archimedes, 11, 75, 75n2
Aristotle, 20, 104
Auger, Pierre, 20, 20n8, 25n14, 55, 107
Avogadro, Armadeo de, 21

Baer, Karl Ernst von, 15
Beeley, Philip, 75n3, 107
Bernoulli, Daniel, 35
Bohr, Neils, 2n2, 104
Boltzmann, Ludwig, 21
Bolzano, Bernhard, 90
Borges, Jorge Luis, 68n10, 76n6, 107
Brandon, Robert N., 16n2, 107

Cardwell, D. S. C., 43n15, 107
Cicero, 76n6, 107
Comte, Auguste, 20, 22, 102n4
Couturat, Louis, 76n7, 107

Darwin, Charles, 15, 43n15
David, Paul A., 64n8, 107
Descartes, René, 11, 46, 76
Dickinson, Jason, 97n2

Dolby, R. G. A., 24n12, 107
Doyle, A. Conan, 47n2, 107
Duhem, Pierre Maurice, 1, 2, 3n3, 105, 108
Dupré, John, 24n13, 108

Eberharter, Veronica, 66n9, 71n13, 108
Eddington, Arthur, 76n6, 108
Einstein, Albert, 79
Euclid, 11, 13n2, 108
Ewell, Raymond H., 55

Fechner, Gustav T., 29, 38, 38n10
Ferrater-Mora, José, 59
Flint, Robert, 20n7, 108, 23n11
Frege, Gottlob, 90

Galton, Francis, 61, 62n4
George, William, 42n12, 51n11, 108
Gibbon, Edward, 29–46, 35n5, 54, 54n19, 61, 73, 105, 108
Glass, Bentley, 55, 63, 63n7, 108
Goffin, William, 70n12, 108
Gore, George, 42n12, 108

Heath, T. C., 75n2, 108
Holland, John H., 15n2, 108
Holub, H. W., 66n9, 71n13, 108